THE RIDE
of a LIFETIME

THE RIDE
of a LIFETIME

Doing Business the Orange
County Choppers Way

PAUL TEUTUL, Sr.
with Mark Yost

WILEY

John Wiley & Sons, Inc.

For general information on our other products and services or for technical support, please contact our Customer Care Department within the United States at (800) 762-2974, outside the United States at (317) 572-3993 or fax (317) 572-4002.

Wiley also publishes its books in a variety of electronic formats. Some content that appears in print may not be available in electronic books. For more information about Wiley products, visit our web site at www.wiley.com.

ISBN: 978-0-470-44997-4

Printed in the United States of America.

10 9 8 7 6 5 4 3

To all the small business owners out there who are struggling like I once did.

Contents

I have seen every episode of *American Chopper*. I have seen the show change, grow, and experiment. I have watched bikes being built for an amusement park, a helicopter company, a truck company, a car company, a snow cone company, a heavy equipment procurement company, a sound system company, a bowling company, Bill Murray, Billy Joel, some magician nobody ever heard of, people who wrote in asking for a bike, the New York Giants, the New York Jets, firemen, veterans wounded in Iraq, a professional golfer, Russell Crowe, Jay Leno, a camping store, some blowhard in Minnesota who builds theme restaurants, weight lifter thugs, the Yankees, the University of Michigan, a widow. You see where this is going. Soon we will all have a custom-built Orange County Chopper chopper. I have ridden three of these bikes—one time with Sylvester Stallone, Bruce Willis, and the Teutuls, through midtown Manhattan in the rain. I have seen the shop change from warehouse to extra-cool 100,000-square-foot World Headquarters. I have seen the staff change. What happened to the first paint guy? Is Nub still around? I was very upset when Vinnie left; I still don't know the full story there. Cody vanished, no word, no trace. That didn't bother me. I grew concerned when, during contract negotiations, Mikey announced he wasn't ``cut out for the business.'' What is he cut out for? I know there is a sister who may be a nurse. I know there is a brother who runs a steel business. I know Senior has a second wife and two large dogs. One misbehaves (a dog, not the wife). He also has a collection of miniature farm animals. How creepy is that? I was worried the poorly trained dog might go crazy and eat the tiny animals. I am also worried about Senior's glaucoma. I like Junior. I like Rick. I like the bald guy with the big voice. I like Lee the new guy. I like Jim Quinn (I guess) though I'm waiting for him to go nuts and explode. I have, even in a very small almost immeasurable way, started to like Jason. Though believe me it wouldn't break my heart if he went to work in the gift shop with Senior's muscle-bound jughead gym buddy.

I've watched them travel to Europe, South America, South Africa, and Australia. I don't like the producer Craig Piligian. I think the guy is a haircut. But I do like that he brought these people to my life. I get angry when there are no new shows. I love the new 50-billion-ton press. I like the Flow Jet. I don't like the hijinks. It's just a matter of time until someone loses a foot.

So what's the deal? Well, I love watching motorcycles being built. I could watch that all day, all week. They could build the same bike over and over and over. Fine with me. I can't get enough. I'm like a dog staring at the refrigerator door. My girlfriend doesn't seem to get this. I gave up trying to articulate my love for this show. I don't get why she enjoys shopping for purses.

So is it the bikes? Yeah, kind of. But over the years something else has happened. I envy this family. They get to spend their time together, good or bad. They love what they do. They scream and throw things and get their feelings hurt, but they also experience the family structure at its highest functioning purpose. Love and support. Few families grow together in this way. That's why I watch. I want to be in this family. My son and I. I want us to be Teutuls and build motorcycles. There, now you know. I'm insane.

—Dave Letterman

ACKNOWLEDGMENTS

*T*here's not enough space (or time) to thank all of the people who have helped me over the past 30 years. You'll meet many of them as you read this book, but there are countless others whose advice, guidance, and honesty helped to make me who and what I am today. To the business partners, suppliers, distributors, and employees who have been a friend to Orange County Ironworks and Orange County Choppers, I thank you all for the part you played in the triumph of these businesses. Whether it was a little piece of advice you gave me or a lesson you helped me learn, some of which ended up in this book, it all contributed to my becoming the successful businessman that I am today.

As for the folks who currently work for me, I'd like to say thanks for coming in every day and working so hard to make Orange County Choppers the extraordinary business it is today—especially Steve Moreau, Scott Amann, Ron Salsbury, Michele Paolella, Joe Puliafico, and Rick Petko. I'd also like to acknowledge Craig Piligian.

I want to thank my publisher, John Wiley & Sons, for believing in this book, and especially Matthew Holt and Shannon Vargo for their outstanding direction and guidance. And to Mark Yost, for helping me to translate my years of experience into something that will provide readers with a way to reach their dreams and goals.

And I have to thank my family—especially my sons Paulie and Michael, who are still involved with Orange County Choppers today.

My name is Paul Teutul Sr. No middle name. My parents couldn't be bothered.

Many of you are probably reading this book because you know me from the television show *American Chopper*, which is about my current business, Orange County Choppers. Yes, we're famous, we're on TV, and people recognize us everywhere we go.

But most everything I am telling you in this book, most everything I learned about running a successful business, I learned from working 28 years in the iron business. Is it applicable to the motorcycle business and did those same principles help Orange County Choppers become a huge success? Certainly. But my point is this: I didn't learn these things in some glamorous business like Orange County Choppers. I learned them in the iron business. It's a tough business. Probably a lot like yours.

I say this for a number of reasons. The business examples and principles in this book can be applied to almost any business. I don't care what it is—software design, corner garage, a mom-and-pop corner convenience store, or a Fortune 500 corporation. Furthermore, I don't want you to be sitting there thinking that because you don't have a show on television, or because people don't recognize you wherever you go, these principles aren't going to work for you. They will.

Wherever you've seen me, I want you to forget what you know about me. The Paul Teutul Sr. you see on television and elsewhere is only a small part of who I am. Yes, I'm that guy, but I'm also a businessman who runs a multimillion-dollar corporation that I built from the ground up with my own two hands.

Over the past two decades, I also beat alcoholism and drug addiction. I defied a lifetime of skeptics who said I'd amount to nothing. And I proved wrong those who said I'd never make it. Along the way, I learned a few things about passion, perseverance, deal making, employee relations, and, yes, the fact that I don't know everything and can't do everything.

That is what this book is all about—how an average guy without much opportunity or resources followed his dreams and clawed his way up the ladder of success. By following my dream and sticking to my principles, I've created one of the most recognized brands in the custom motorcycle market. And I've earned a pretty good living along the way.

How did I do it? By following what I like to call Teutul's Tenets of Doing Business. They're simple, straightforward, and can be applied to almost any business.

Partnerships. I've been in a number of internal business partnerships over the years and it has been my experience that they don't work because you lose control over half the business, which makes you semi-powerless. More importantly, to be successful, partnerships often require you to dilute your vision. No two people are ever going to think exactly alike on every subject. So at some point, you have to compromise your vision.

Passion. This is the main ingredient in being successful. If you don't have a passion for what you're doing, then you shouldn't be doing it.

Perseverance. Perseverance is essential to being successful in anything you do, not just in business. If you fold under pressure, or lack the drive to push your way through the tough times, you're going to lose the challenges you face. And, believe me, there will be a lot of 'em.

Stick to Your Commitments. If you make a commitment to someone, you'd better be able to stand behind it. This goes for your suppliers, your customers, your employees, and anyone else you do business with. One way to ensure that you can deliver on your promises is to always understand what you're getting into and make sure that you can live up to it. If you don't, you're going to be in big trouble.

Welcome Change. No matter how long you've been in business or how successful you've been, you have to believe that you can still teach an old dog new tricks. If you don't adapt to changes, positive changes, you're just hurting yourself.

Never Sell Out. You should be willing to change to make your business better, but never sell out. There's a difference.

Be an Example. If you're going to talk the talk, you'd better walk the walk. I wouldn't ask any of my employees to do anything that I wouldn't do myself. I like to remind guys in the shop from time to time that I used to do this or that.

Surround Yourself with Good People. You're only as good as the people around you. Your employees can make you or break you, and you need your employees not only to be successful, but to expand their knowledge and expertise as well.

Learn to Trust Others. When I first started out in business, I did everything myself. That's because I was always concerned that the job be done right.

But doing everything yourself can work for only so long. **Don't Let Pride Get in the Way.** If you surround yourself with good people, you eventually realize that you're not always the smartest guy in the room. If you make a mistake, be big enough to admit it, even to employees.

Stay Organized. My experience is that if you're organized, you save steps. And every step you take costs you money—so in order to be productive you need to have a plan and you need to be organized.

Be efficient in everything you do.

Take Care of Your Employees. My employees have never been just employees to me. They're part of a family. I'm a big believer in giving credit where credit is due. In order to build morale, you need to pat your employees on the back every once in awhile.

Running a Family Business. Many of the most successful businesses today are family businesses. Unfortunately, they can be both a blessing and a curse, because as hard as you might try, you can never treat family like just another employee.

Never Back Down. When you have a dream and a vision for a business, you have to stick to it, even when others are telling you you're headed in the wrong direction.

Never Stop Halfway or Lower Your Standards. As long as you're in business, those two motivating factors should be, too.

Learn from Your Mistakes. Nobody's perfect; we all make errors in judgment in business and in life. You'll learn more from the experience of making that mistake and suffering its consequences than from hearing about it from someone else.

Be Humble. This is probably hard to believe from someone like me, but you have to be humble; it means being smart enough to learn from people who know more than you.

Give Back. Making money and being successful is great, but it doesn't give you the same satisfaction that you get when you give back to people less fortunate. The return will be far more than what you give.

Always Follow Your Dream. It sounds simple, but you can never lose sight of your dream, no matter how long you have had it or how far off it seems.

So that's basically it. A short list of the principles and ideals that I've followed as I built Orange County Choppers from a hobby in my basement to the brand that it is today. As the title says, it's been *The Ride of a Lifetime*. So hang on.

THE RIDE
of a **LIFETIME**

1

Choices

If you take one lesson away from this book, let it be this: Your past does not dictate your destiny. You have choices in life. The sooner you realize that—and start making the right choices—the sooner you'll be a success. I've learned many lessons over the years, in both business and in life. If I had known sooner that I'd had more choices—was not a prisoner of my past—I would have been much more successful much sooner.

So if you're picking up this book because you're a small-business owner, or you are thinking about starting your own business, or you are frustrated that you haven't become the success that you hoped to, and feel like you're destined to make the same mistakes you've made in the past, let me tell you this: It doesn't have to be that way. You have choices, just as I did over the past 30-odd years.

In fact, if I chose one word—one theme, if you will—to describe my life—how it started, how it evolved, and what it ultimately became—it would be "choices."

As a kid growing up, I basically didn't have any choices. None. Zero. Zilch. It was that simple. My dad made all the decisions for us, in nearly every aspect of our lives. He told us what time to get up, what to eat for breakfast, and what time to go to bed. In between, we had very few choices. If we went to the store to buy school clothes, my dad would pick them out for us. He'd say, "These are the shoes I'm buying you, and you're going to wear them."

Even when I was making my own money, my dad continued to tell me what I was going to buy. A good example is my first car: It was a 1964 Dodge Dart with the Slant-Six engine in it. I hated that car. I thought it was the ugliest car in the world. I really wanted a fast car. A cool car. Like a '55 or '56 Chevy. But my father wouldn't let me buy one. And in my house, that was that. Once the old man spoke, that was the way it was going to be.

As I got older, my choices didn't get much better. They were extremely limited, mainly because of my upbringing, my background, and my own sense of self-worth. I don't think anyone had high expectations for me, including myself. My whole childhood basically set me up to be dead or in prison, especially coming from the background that I came from. And, sadly, that's what happened to a lot of my friends. Worse yet, for the longest time I believed that the path I was on was the only option I had.

It was only after I realized that the world was full of choices that my life began to change. I realized that I had a choice of who I was, what I stood for, and what my life could be. Then I realized that my possibilities for success—in business as well as my personal life— were limited only by my own drive, ambition, and willingness to work hard. Working hard was never an issue for me. I'd been working hard my whole life. What changed everything for me was finally realizing that I could work hard toward the goals and dreams that mattered most to me. But I'm getting ahead of myself.

I can honestly tell you that you can overcome anything that life hands you, because that's what I've been doing most of my life: overcoming and exceeding everyone's expectations that they had for me and that I initially had for myself. I don't think it's a stretch for me to say that I've been knocked down a lot of times in my life, but I was always able to pick myself up each time, and put one foot in front of the other. For the most part, I've succeeded at that.

Against All Odds

Why the long odds against me? From the day I was born—May 1, 1949, in Yonkers, New York—no one ever really expected me to amount to much. Not my parents. Not my teachers. Nor anyone else for that matter. That's because my childhood was very dysfunctional and violent. I grew up in a household where my mother was always belittling my father—and because of that my father abused me and my four sisters because he was so frustrated by our mother. It really was that bad.

There was no support in my house. It was not a loving experience. There was just anger. No one ever said, "I love you." The word "love" was never mentioned. Everything that was done was done with brute force. And if my parents made a mistake or gave us a beating, there was no such thing as saying "I'm sorry."

Having grown up in that environment, naturally I became a bit of a rebel. I didn't conform to the rules of school or society. That's because when you grow up like that, you don't know what normal is. You don't know if other families are like that, or you're just different. You just try and make it through every day.

As far as having any kind of role model when I was a kid, the only person I can say that I actually looked up to—because I didn't look up to my mother or my father—was my Uncle Emil. But even he wasn't the ideal role model when you think about the types of people who are often considered positive influences in a young kid's life. He was a drunk and a gambler. But he at least showed an interest in me, and that was more than I could say for most of the other people in my life.

But even my uncle wasn't around for very long. When I was seven years old, he died. He was killed in a car accident while bookies he owed money to were chasing him. He had been drinking, flipped his car over, and was killed. That was the most traumatic thing that ever happened to me in my life up to that point.

The thing I remember most about my time with Uncle Emil is that we would build scale models together—cars and vintage military biplanes, mostly. He especially liked building the planes. And these were real models, not the kind you find today where you just snap together a few parts. These models had lots of tiny parts, and you had to put every one of them together. Before putting them together, you had to sand off the rough edges on each piece and paint them. You even had to glue on some of the engine components.

It seemed like a small thing at the time, but this was the first time that I learned to take pride in my work and pay attention to detail. Building these models was also my first passion in life. I had not realized that until just recently, but it was true.

Shop Kid

Because my family was not the least bit encouraging, when I got older, I wasn't very good in school. So like a lot of troubled kids growing up in the 1950s and '60s, I was funneled into shop class. In New York State they have a fancy name for it: BOCES, which stands for Bureau of Cooperative Educational Services. But it was basically shop class, and it was where they sent all the kids they didn't have much hope for.

I didn't learn much there, except how to steal lunches out of the other kids' lockers. But I did learn how to weld, a skill that would help me start my own business one day. Other than welding, the only thing school did for me was allow me to have fun with my friends and be around good-looking women. Otherwise, I thought school was a total waste of time for me.

When I was about 10 years old, I moved on from model planes and started to get interested in cars. I could probably identify three-quarters of the cars that were on the road. I could spot most of them just by looking at their headlights. From a block away, I could tell you the difference between a '55 and '56 Ford, or a '53 Olds and a Buick Roadmaster.

This interest in cars would later become the passion that fueled me, but you don't know that at that age. And thinking about it today, no one who knew me then could honestly say that they saw my interest and knowledge in cars as something that would lead to the successful business I have today. That's because with no one around to support or encourage me to excel at something I really cared about and liked, it remained just a passing hobby.

But here's the funny thing and, ultimately, one of the reasons why I think I succeeded. Although I had little ambition early in life, I worked very hard from about the time I was 10 or 11—hard labor mostly. When I wasn't in school, I was doing grunt work for my parents around the house. My grandfather liked to put me to work, too. He always had a pick or a shovel in my hand, making me do hard labor around his house.

I always had a job in high school. I worked at a few gas stations. During the summer, I worked for a furniture-moving company. But it wasn't some sort of deep-seated work ethic. My parents never said, "Son, you have to get a job because it'll make you a better person" or put a roof over my head someday. Yeah, I worked hard, and I took pride in my work. But the real reason I worked so hard was that as long as I was living at home, and I was old enough to work, I had to pay rent. I wish I could say that it was something more than that, something deeper and more meaningful, but it wasn't. I was simply expected to pull my weight, no matter what.

While that may sound harsh, I'm proud to say that nothing was ever given to me. Everything I've ever achieved in life has been through my own hard work. If I had a car, it was because I had worked hard, saved up for it, and bought that car with my own money.

No Regrets

That basically describes the first 18 years of my life. When I was about 15, I started drinking and doing drugs. And everyone around me expected me to fail. I was a prisoner of my own demons. It would take me 20 years to shake off those demons. I don't regret growing up like that. I'm not bitter about it. As bad as it was, that upbringing made me who I am today. And I honestly don't think I'd be who— or what—I am today if I hadn't gone through all that.

I don't regret being addicted to drugs and alcohol for 20 years either. I do have regrets for what my alcoholism and drug addiction did to other people, especially my family. But for me, the hardship and the struggles became my inspiration. I began drinking when I was 15 and didn't become sober until I was 35. In between, I wrecked a lot of cars and a lot of lives, including my own. But once I got through all that, sobered up, and realized that I had the ability to change my life, it became a whole new world for me.

Unfortunately, it would take me until I was 35 years old to come to that realization. That's because when you come from a family like mine and you're an alcoholic and a drug addict, you really have no self-worth. You really don't like yourself. This is especially true when you're an alcoholic and taking drugs. You really don't have a choice. You can say to yourself, "I'm not going too drink today." Well, too fucking bad, pal, you're drinking today. You're a prisoner.

When I graduated (miraculously) from high school in 1969, everyone was worried about being drafted for the war. Vietnam was in full swing, and a lot of my friends were getting drafted. So I decided to join the Merchant Marine. "How hard could it be?" I thought. Get on a boat, work hard, and see the world. It sounded like a good idea to me. I'd been working hard most of my life, and anywhere was better than where I was.

But I firmly believe that life is what you make of it, and at this point in my life, I wasn't prepared to make much of it. The Merchant Marine turned out to be exactly what I'd expected it to be. We got on a boat, worked hard, and saw the world. And in between, we did some really great drugs.

But looking back on it now, I realize that some important things happened to me in the Merchant Marine. One was boot camp. When I joined the Merchant Marine, it was the first year they had implemented boot camp. And it was for three months, not six or eight weeks, like in the Army. I joined with my best friend, Clem Lawler, and he lasted a week. He went home because of personal problems.

I'm not ashamed to say that I wanted to go home, too. While going into the Merchant Marine seemed like no big deal, it was a very big deal for me. I was a young guy, 18 years old, and I'd never been away from home before. After that first week, I wanted to go home so badly I could taste it. But somewhere deep inside myself, I said, "You have to get through this challenge." I did. And here's how I did it.

I remember being by myself one night. There was a long stretch of open space between my barracks and the beach. I don't know why, but I decided that I was going to run as fast as I could to the beach. And I wasn't going to stop, no matter how painful it was. More importantly, I said to myself, "If I can run to the water without stopping, no matter how much it hurts and how much I want to stop, then I can make it through boot camp."

I did it, and that was the end of the struggle of whether or not I was going to make it through boot camp. It may seem like a small thing, but it was important. Because looking back on it now, I recognize that I was challenging myself to succeed for the first time in my life. I was trying to prove to myself—and to others, I guess— that I wasn't going to be a failure. That I could beat the odds and not be that loser that everyone expected me to be.

Was it the last time that I failed? Of course not. I was 18 when I completed boot camp and, as I've said, I didn't get clean and sober until I was 35. For most of the next 17 years, I was often my own worst enemy. I was the obstacle that kept me from believing in myself, executing my vision, and becoming the success that I am today.

But making that run at boot camp was an important first step toward changing me. It was an important step in leaving behind the person that everyone expected to fail and becoming the success that I am today. I didn't realize it then, but I was learning that I could challenge myself and succeed. It would take a while for the message to sink in, but this was an important step on that road of transformation.

Back Home Again

After I got out of the Merchant Marine, I came home and married a girl I had dated a few times in high school, Paula Leonardo. A year later, my first son, Paul, was born.

As for work, I bounced around from job to job. I'd learned welding in BOCES and was fairly good at it. I started working for a few businesses around Rockland County. But what I learned during this period in my life was that I didn't like working for someone else. I didn't like taking orders and being told how to do something. I had my own ways and my own ideas. Having a boss just completely rubbed me the wrong way.

The last job I had working for someone else was with my brother-in-law. I worked for him for four months in 1974, and then decided to go into business by myself. I was 24 years old. I was still a drunk and a drug abuser. But I scraped up the cash and bought a truck—a '66 International—from my father. I bought a welding rig from a friend of mine who was going to jail. What was my business plan? No fucking clue. But I'd never had trouble making money. That's because I was a hard worker. So my business plan was nothing more than "Try and make money. Try and be successful."

To this day, I really don't know where I got this solid work ethic. I've just always had it. Maybe it's because I knew that no one else was going to take care of me. Maybe it's because my grandfather was a workaholic. He worked seven days a week. He built entire houses by himself. He was an animal. But I don't think that I got his work ethic, because I really don't remember what it was, except that he was always working.

I think I always worked and paid my bills because I knew that no one was going to do it for me. If I failed, then I failed. I now know that what really drove me this whole time was my desire not to fail, because I wanted to prove everybody else wrong. I had to prove that I wasn't a failure. That's because it was drilled into me—both consciously and unconsciously—from the time that I was a little kid that I wasn't ever going to be anything. People had no expectations for me.

I even remember teachers in school telling me, "You're never going to amount to anything." That's not merely my impression of what they thought of me; teachers actually said that to me. And I think it's something that stays with you. Eventually, there comes a time in your life when you've got to make a decision: Are you or are you not going to be a failure? And, if not, what are you going to do?

I chose to challenge myself again by going into business for myself. I chose to go into business because I wanted to be my own boss and knew that I could be successful as my own boss. Once you do that, everything rests on you. There's nobody else there to blame. I knew I wanted to have the freedom to be self-employed. At the time, I thought that meant that you could do what you wanted, when you wanted, at any given time. Unfortunately, I learned the hard way that wasn't the way it worked.

Moreover, I used my own business as a shield for my alcoholism and drug abuse. I figured that if I had my own business, and I was paying the bills, it didn't matter if I was drunk and stoned in the bar at three o'clock in the afternoon. "Hey man," I'd say, "I have my own business." And that, I thought, made it okay to do whatever I wanted. That was basically my business model for the next 11 years.

I hired employees who I knew from drinking with them. My business partner, Fred Gerini, was one of them. Doing a few shots before going to the job site, drinking your lunch, and heading to the liquor store at 2 P.M. to get a couple cases of beer and a couple bottles of Black Velvet seemed normal to me. I'm not telling you all this to make you feel sorry for me. I'm telling it to you to illustrate how lost I was. And if somebody as lost and fucked up as me can get their life together, and be the success that I am today, then anyone can do it. You just have to believe in yourself and your vision.

You have to believe that no matter what your background is, no matter what people in your past told you that you were supposed to be, you can make your future whatever you want it to be. It's just a matter of first realizing that you have choices, and then making the right ones. Unfortunately for me, it would be another 11 years before I realized that. But I'd learn some valuable lessons along the way.

2

No Thanks, Pardner

or me, there's a very simple reason why partnerships are a bad idea. In a partnership, you lose control over half the business. Partnerships also often lead to conflict, which inevitably leads to a stalemate. And if you're in a stalemate, your business is not moving forward. And that's not good.

I know there have been some very successful partnerships over the years: Ernst & Young, Pratt & Whitney, Procter & Gamble. But with a headstrong guy like me, there's always going to be a difference of opinion between me and the people I work with. That's just the way it is. And if you're wondering whose opinion usually wins out in my shop, just ask my sons.

To me, the question is, why have a partner when you can hire and pay somebody good money to do the same thing? The benefit is that there are no obligations there. If it doesn't work out, you can go your separate ways, hopefully not have any hard feelings, and move on to the next prospect. Partnerships can be successful, but you can also feel like you're boxed in. If one person doesn't agree with you on something, that can put you in a position of powerlessness. And that's not good for the partners or the business.

Unfortunately, it took me a long time—and a major life change—to learn all of this. So consider yourself lucky. If you're reading this book before you've made a lot of these mistakes, you're saving yourself a lot of headaches. But I'm getting ahead of myself again.

Some Tough Lessons

So there I was. Twenty-four years old. Out of the Merchant Marine. Married. With a son. And back in Orange County,

New York. Despite everyone's prediction that I would be a total failure, I had started my own business, Paul's Welding, when I got out of the Merchant Marine. It was nothing more than me, a truck, and a single welding unit. But it was, in most people's eyes, nothing short of a miracle. If you had asked anyone who knew me in high school where I'd end up, their answer would have been dead or in jail. And for the next decade, I was able to prove them all wrong. I not only earned a living and provided for my growing family, but I was even able to expand my business. To anyone looking in from the outside, I was a success. But on the inside, I was a total wreck.

I worked by myself for a few months and then went to work for my brother-in-law in his steel shop. This was a valuable lesson, because I quickly realized that I didn't want to work for and take orders from someone else for the rest of my life. So I opened up a small shop in 1973 with a friend of mine, Fred Gerini, from Brooklyn. We called it P&F Ironworks. Basically, I thought I needed a partner because I was the guy with the balls, not the guy with the brains. I thought I needed someone who had more experience in the iron and steel business than I did. I felt that the combination of Fred's brains and my balls would work well. And for a while, it did.

Fred had already been in business, working for other people. And he had worked alongside me in my brother-in-law's iron shop. That's how I met him. So when my brother-in-law went out of business in 1973, we had no choice but to leave there and do something else. That's how we went into business as P&F Ironworks.

We started out doing piecemeal welding jobs for businesses in the area—mostly welding farm equipment. But we quickly realized we had to get more clients and expand into different types of work. Welding farm equipment wasn't going to pay the bills. So we started to work with a guy named Bill Belmonte. He was a jobber, meaning that he found jobs for people. He worked with a lot of the contractors and developers in the area, and they would ask him to contract out portions of their jobs. So he'd get a job from them, call us up, send us out to the worksite to do the job, and take 10 percent. He also advertised in the local Penny Saver.

Working with Bill, we were working mostly with new housing developments, putting the ornamental ironwork on porches. These were big developments that were being built to attract all the people who were fleeing the skyrocketing real estate prices in New York City. Orange County is only about 45 minutes north of the city, and it's also the farthest out that cops, firefighters, and other city employees can live and still meet the city's residency requirements. So these developers were building 20 or 30 houses at a time, and they were booming. It was a good business. As soon as the developer put a porch on a house, we'd go out to the site and install the ironwork. It was that simple.

But after a while, we realized we still weren't really making any money. Yes, Bill kept us busy with steady work, but we spent a lot of time going back and forth between the job site and the shop. We'd have to go out and do all of the measuring and make sure we came back with the right materials. Over time, it became clear to us that this partnership wasn't working. This was the first time I realized that maybe partnerships weren't such a good idea.

So Fred and I began doing some of the things Bill Belmonte was doing. We started advertising in the Penny Saver and finding these jobs ourselves. It really wasn't that hard. Furthermore, we realized that by bidding the jobs ourselves, we had a better sense of what the work would entail, how long it would take us, and what kind of materials we'd need. And we weren't paying Bill his 10 percent commission. That made a world of difference, and the business became much more profitable for us. But six months after we stopped working with Bill, my partnership with Fred went bad.

Goodbye, Fred

Up to this point, Fred was just like me. We were drinking buddies. And for a while, it worked out pretty well. We could easily handle these contracting jobs at the new housing developments in Orange County. We knew exactly what we had to do, we'd show up to the job site, knock it out, and then we'd go to the bar and party.

Then Fred met a girl. She was extremely spiritual. Don't ask me what religion she was or what denomination. All I know is that she spent a lot of time in church. That's where Fred wanted to be, too, and that was a problem. The reason Fred and I worked so well together for those first six months is that we were of the same mindset. When we weren't drinking, we were totally focused on the business. But after he met this girl, he went from being totally dedicated to the business to having an attitude of "I have a girl now and I want to spend most of my time with her and in church." He stopped showing up and wasn't as interested in work as he had been. That was his choice, but it wasn't the choice for me.

That's not the kind of focus you're looking for in a partner. For me, it was always about teamwork, the passion to succeed, and being your own boss. We were just trying to build the business so that, basically, we didn't have to depend on anyone else to survive. When Fred decided he wanted to spend more time in church and less time at work, that was fine with me. I realized—for the first time—that I was much better off working by myself.

Then disaster struck. I was working in the shop by myself, making railings for a porch at the housing development I was working on. In the back of the shop, there was a 40-gallon paint tank we would dip the rails in after they were fabricated. I was grinding some rails, a spark flew into the paint tank, and it caught on fire. Within an hour, the shop burned to the ground, with almost everything I owned. That's when I let Fred go. He wanted out anyway, which was fine with me.

A New Beginning

After the fire, I went into the building and rummaged through the debris to salvage what I could. I went home, bringing what I could to my garage, cleaned it up, and I never missed a beat. Through it all, I never missed a delivery to my customers. I credit my old work ethic. It kicked in, and I survived a catastrophe that would have destroyed a lot of other guys. Another lesson that perseverance and hard work always pays off. Back then, I wasn't so clear-headed, but I realize all this now.

As soon as I got my business up and running again in another shop, I still hadn't learned my lesson about partnerships, so I hired another partner, John Grosso—another one of my drinking buddies. John had also worked in the steel shop with my brother-in-law. He was a production guy. And, like me, he was an animal when it came to work. We both had the same focus and mindset.

We knew that the quicker we finished a job, the sooner we could get to the bar and start drinking. That motivated us to develop a system that helped us be as efficient as possible, get the job done, and get to drinking. When John and I pulled up to a job site, we knew exactly what we had to do. We didn't even have to speak to each other. As soon as the truck stopped, we'd get out and go to work. It was pretty impressive. Too bad the motivation was all wrong.

He'd start pulling the rails off the truck, while I went onto the porch and started marking the holes. We were like lightning. We'd be out of there in 15 minutes. On bigger jobs that would take most contractors a day or more, we'd be out of there in half that time. It truly was amazing. And for a long time, it worked great. We were one hell of a team. Then, I was the partner who changed his mind.

Sobering Up

I remember the day exactly. It was January 7, 1985—11 years after going into business together. Twenty years of hard drinking and partying since the age of 15 had finally caught up with me. My body was literally falling apart. I was coughing up blood. Over the years, I had wrecked a dozen or more cars. On the weekends, I would wake up and not know where I was or how I'd gotten there.

So on January 7, 1985, I decided that I'd either have to sober up, or die. I chose to die. I told my wife, Paula, who had been through so much with me and should be nominated for sainthood, that as much as I would like to get sober, I couldn't. So my only choice was to die.

Somehow, she talked me into going into rehab, something I thought I'd never do. But I wanted to have one last good drunk. So the day before I was set to go into rehab, I got totally plastered. I drank a half-gallon of wine, a pint of brandy, and I took six Valiums. I woke up the next morning completely hung over. I had promised my wife that I would go, but I just couldn't. And you want to know why I couldn't do it? Because I couldn't leave my business. I thought that if I went into rehab that I'd lose everything I'd accomplished up to that point: my business, my customers, my reputation. In my mind, if I went away for 30 days, I thought it would all go away and I'd have to start all over again.

You also have to remember that throughout all my years of drinking and doing drugs, I went to work no matter what: broken arms, smashed fingers, the flu. Even toward the end, when I was spitting up blood, I showed up to work every day. No matter what. So in my mind, I couldn't take 30 days off from work, even if it was the only way to save my life. I couldn't lose everything that I had gained over the past 11 years. There was an uncertainty there that I simply couldn't handle.

But I'm a man of my word. And my word is my ironclad bond, and my vow to my wife had been to get sober, and that was what I was going to do. So instead of checking myself into rehab, I went to an Alcoholics Anonymous (AA) meeting—something I'd said I would never do. For the next nine years, I never missed a meeting. Thankfully, in January 2009, I had been sober for 24 years.

That was the beginning of a whole new life for me. A life that—I finally realized—was full of choices. And one of those choices was not to drink, although it took me a while to figure that out. Once I went to that first AA meeting on January 7, 1985, I never took another drink. But I was tempted every day. That's because I was surrounded by drinkers. My partner, John Grosso, and all the guys who worked for us were all boozers. I was the only guy who had decided to sober up, so there was constant pressure on me to drink. I would be on the job site with these guys, or in the truck, trying not to drink, and they'd be passing a bottle of whiskey or downing a case of beer. It was a challenge every day.

For a while, I thought I could deal with it. I thought I could be around them and not drink. They'd send me out for a case of beer and a bottle of Black Velvet at 2 P.M. And, like a dummy, I'd go get it for them. I didn't think that just because I had stopped drinking that I couldn't hang out with my drinking buddies.

About a year into AA, I was not drinking, but it was still a daily struggle. It was one of the hardest things I'd ever done not to grab hold of that bottle that was being passed around the truck and take a swig. I didn't know how long I could keep saying "no."

Then a guy in AA told me something that saved my life. He said, "If you don't drink just for today, you may be dead tomorrow. So just worry about getting through today." That was it for me. I finally got it. I understood that I couldn't worry about being sober a month or a year or five years from now. It was a day-to-day struggle. And if you simply don't drink for today, then you're winning the battle. It sounds so simple—"Just don't drink for today"—but it saved my life.

A New Life

When I stopped drinking, it opened up a whole new life for me—a life full of choices—and, for the first time ever, I was in charge. It was also the end of the life I had been living. The life of drinking and drugs that had ruled my life and held me back professionally. And that meant the end of another partnership.

That's because John Grosso had not only been my business partner, but he had also been my drinking buddy. After we'd bang out a job, we'd spend the afternoon on a bar stool somewhere, talking about all the great things we were going to do with the business. Of course, we never did them. That's because it took all of our energy to just get out of bed in the morning, get to the job site, and then get to the bar. It was a vicious cycle.

When I got sober in 1985, John tried to get sober, too. Unfortunately, he didn't make it. One year after getting sober, I finally told all the guys that there was no more drinking in the shop, no more drinking in the truck, and no more drinking on the job site. They had to stop. It was my choice, and I embraced the fact that for the first time in my life I had control over making that decision. Needless to say, most of my employees who were my old drinking buddies disappeared. They weren't going to tolerate that. Old Paulie simply wasn't as fun as he used to be. Maybe not, but I was a hell of a lot more focused. And it started to show.

Two years after getting sober, I built my own shop. John Grosso still worked for me, but he was no longer my partner. He was just an employee. I tried to reach out to him. I would say, "Listen, John, if I can do it, anybody can do it." I thought I could get through to him. I drank with this guy for 10 years. In fact, I drank harder than he did. He would go to a couple of AA meetings, get sober for a week, and then start drinking again. It finally got to a point where he was still coming to work drunk. Eventually, I had to say, "You can't come here, you can't be drinking, and you can't be drunk." I told him, "Either get sober or you have to leave."

He chose to leave. It was one of the hardest things I ever had to do, but it was a sign of my own personal growth in my sobriety. John moved to Florida and went to work for my brother-in-law again, but he came back to Orange County about six months later. He was dying. His liver was gone. A few months later, he died. He was just 35. That's an interesting number: 35. Only one in 35 people end up staying sober. I guess I was one of the lucky ones—and still am.

I was sober, I was thinking straight, focused and driven, but I still shunned partnerships. That's because I realized that when I was drinking, the alcohol and the drugs blurred my vision. But being with a partner who doesn't share your vision can do the same thing. That's why I don't do partnerships. Not then, not now.

But as my business took off like never before, I realized that I couldn't do everything on my own. Two years after getting sober, I bought a piece of property on Stone Castle Road in Rock Tavern, New York, and built a new shop. I also started diversifying. The residential work was slowing down, so I moved into commercial work. I became a fabricator, started to develop relationships with contractors, and accumulated quite a bit of work. Again, it's about realizing that I had choices. I wasn't locked into just one type of business.

Because I was now thinking clearly, I had the good sense to make the building about twice as big as it needed to be at the time. I say "at the time" because in the span of just a few years, I ended up tripling the size of the facility and renting another building down the street. As my business grew and diversified, I went from just four employees to more than 70. And it's all because I was sober, thinking clearly, and driven. More importantly, I was able to take that drive that was always there and apply it in a positive way. Before, my drive was put into just showing up for work. "What can be wrong with me?" I used to think. "I get up and go to work every day." But a lot of energy was being wasted.

Now, I don't want you to finish this chapter by thinking that all of my experiences with partnerships have been bad. That's simply not true. My issue is exclusively with having a partner *inside* the business. I don't want someone who, as a partner, has the same input as me into the direction and growth of the company. I'm totally against those kinds of partnerships, for all the reasons I've listed so far.

What I am not against are partnerships *outside* the business, because that would be simply impossible. As focused and driven as I was after I sobered up, I quickly learned that I had to make limited partnerships with people who could help me achieve my dreams and my goals. A clear example of that was a partnership I started back in the early 1970s, when I first started building custom bikes in my basement.

Ted Doering had a company in Newburgh, New York, called V-Twin Manufacturing. Back then, he was selling custom and vintage motorcycle parts out of his barn. When I needed a part, I would walk into his place—he'd have a piece of straw in his mouth, the floor was nothing but packed dirt—and we'd bargain for parts. Today, he's one of the largest distributors of aftermarket motorcycle parts in the world.

Initially, Ted didn't like the fact that I was going to take his parts—like a gas tank—and cut them up to make them look the way I wanted. But we eventually became friends. More than that, he was an early mentor. Ted was the guy I would reach out to when I would build bikes in my basement for myself, long before I started Orange County Choppers. He was the guy who would point me in the right direction in terms of the parts I needed to build the bike I wanted to create. And because he carried a lot of vintage parts I needed to customize the old-style bikes I liked back then, he was a great partner. I could go into his place and build a whole '57 chopper out of parts. In short, Ted Doering was my first successful business partner.

In the 1970s, I wanted to build a panhead chopper with a Patogh frame, an old-school bike for myself. We'd start at the rear tire and work our way all the way up to the front end. He walked me through the whole thing. That's how I started building the early old-style bikes. Eventually, I didn't need Ted anymore. I had built so many bikes that I could figure it out myself. But he was a good partner and supplied me with most of what I needed in the early days.

From these humble beginnings, I built Orange County Choppers. While it's a hugely successful business, it wouldn't exist without the passion I have for motorcycles. And after having just read the previous chapter, you'll be surprised where I got my passion for customizing old motorcycles.

3

Passion

One of the keys to being successful in business—and in life—is the ability to not only survive a bad experience, but to come out the other side and figure out what you gained from it. For instance, it took me a couple of bad experiences, but I finally realized that partnerships didn't work for me. But the bigger lesson is this: Nothing is ever a total loss or a total waste of time. You have to be able to learn from both your successes and failures if you're going to be successful in business.

What I also learned from my failed partnerships is that they often get in the way of following your real passion in life, because they often require you to make compromises. And if you're going to succeed in business, you must have passion.

Having a passion for what you do, in my opinion, is one of the keys to being successful. If you don't have excitement and enthusiasm for what you're doing, then you shouldn't be doing it. Your passion is what drives you and what makes you strive to be better. If you're passionate about what you're doing, then it's not a job; it's something you love to do.

Finding Your Passion

When you're working, you're either working because you have to or because you want to. Finding your passion makes you want to go to work every day. That's what I learned when I finally found my passion for building bikes. I build them because I want to. It's what drives me, to give 110 percent in everything I do. It's the difference between forcing yourself to do something and wanting to do something. To be successful in business—truly successful—it can't always be about finishing the job and making money. It has to be about doing something that you really love.

So how did I discover my passion for building motorcycles? From my time working with Fred Gerini, my first business partner. As I mentioned, I wasn't what you'd call a gearhead in high school. I liked cars, and I knew a lot about them. But they weren't something I was passionate about. And I barely even looked at motorcycles back then. Yeah, some of the guys in the neighborhood had them, but I didn't grow up in a motorcycle culture. They were there, but I didn't pay much attention to them.

The first time I really began being interested in bikes was when the movie *Easy Rider* came out in 1969. And it wasn't so much about the bikes as it was the sense of freedom that a whole generation of people who saw this movie associated with them. Even though the movie ended tragically, I dreamed of building my own bike one day and riding it around the world. But that's basically where the dream ended. For the time being.

It wasn't until four years later, in 1973, that I rode my first bike. A buddy of mine had a Honda 300 with ape hangers—a style of handlebars where the handgrips are located at a higher position, so as to enable the rider's arms to hang. He picked me up one day and we went cruising. After a while, he pulled over and said, "Wanna drive?" I picked it up right away. Buzzing down Middletown Road, I was hooked.

It wasn't long after that when I bought my first bike, a used '71 Triumph. It was gold and black with streaks of white in it. I'd occasionally take it cruising through Upstate New York, but mostly I just rode it back and forth to work. And I really didn't think about turning it into a chopper with extended front forks or making any other custom modifications to it.

It was at this point that I partnered with Fred Gerini and started P&F Ironworks. Fred was the first Harley guy I ever met. And even though I owned a Triumph, it was the closest thing you could get to a Harley, since they were really expensive back then. And the

Triumph was definitely a step up from the Hondas and Yamahas that were starting to show up on roads.

Fred was a real Harley enthusiast. He had a good friend who was also into Harleys, and these guys were really smart when it came to bikes. They thoroughly understood the mechanics, and they were fairly creative guys when it came to chopping and customizing motorcycles. They had the skills and know-how to do whatever they wanted with a bike.

Being around these guys was one of the most valuable learning experiences for me. Early on, I just stood back and watched, but I paid attention to what they were doing. I knew little or nothing about bikes, except how to ride them. But I was always good mechanically and was a fast learner. They would work in the Ironworks shop on nights and weekends and would do stuff like extend the springers, stretch the frame, and I would watch them do all of this.

Back then, it took a while to build a bike just like they wanted, mainly because they couldn't afford to buy all the parts at once. They'd buy parts at swap meets. The parts they couldn't get—or couldn't afford—they'd make by hand in the shop. But over time, everything would come together and eventually, there would be *the* bike sitting in the shop. It would be everything that they had envisioned it to be. And it was a work of art.

I learned everything there was to know about customizing bikes: the mechanics, design, chroming, accessories. This was, without a doubt, the most important learning period of my life. I not only developed a passion for motorcycles, but I also learned how to take that passion, channel it, and apply it in positive, productive ways. It was this passion, and the ability to use it, that eventually made me a very successful businessperson.

So while Fred was my bar buddy and was with me on that seemingly endless cycle of drinking, I have him to thank for helping me find my passion for bikes. That's what I meant earlier when I said that in order to be successful in business, you have to be able to get through a bad situation and look back and figure out not only what you learned from the failure, but also what you gained from that experience. There's always something to learn from every situation, no matter what business you're in.

Finding My Eye

While Fred helped me discover my passion for bikes, he gave me something much more important: Fred helped me develop my eye for what's important in the design, look, and feel of a motorcycle.

When we'd sit around the shop talking or go to swap meets, Fred used to talk about the lines of a bike. At first, I didn't quite understand why what he was talking about was so important. He explained to me that you could have a thousand different individual parts on a motorcycle, but you don't really notice them unless you get up close to the bike and study it. What catches your eye from afar—and ultimately defines the bike—are the lines. How the bike flows, from the front tire to the rear. How the front wheel lines up with the frame. How the line of the bike flows from the base of the handlebars, across the gas tank, across the seat, to the rear fender.

Another way of saying this is that you shouldn't miss the forest for the trees. In business, that means that you can't be so focused on the minute individual details that you lose sight of the ultimate goal, the finished product. Yes, paying attention to details is important, and ultimately determines the outcome of the larger project or product, but you can never lose sight of that bigger picture. And you must always see the small details not just as themselves, but how they contribute to that bigger picture. End of lecture, and back to the story.

Once I understood what Fred meant when he talked about the lines of a bike, I became more familiar with how to build a bike. I stopped watching and started working with these guys. I quickly realized that I was particularly drawn to the bikes of the 1960s.

Basically, I preferred the old-school choppers to the more modern ones. In fact, they're still my favorite bikes today.

Over time, my passion for motorcycles continued to grow. And it fueled my desire to learn as much as I could about them—even the models I didn't necessarily like. I started buying motorcycle magazines, to learn everything that I could about bikes. After a few years, I had a hall closet stuffed with four tall stacks of motorcycle magazines. At night, I would sit in my living room and go through these magazines. And after I'd gone through them all, I'd start all over again. My wife thought I was nuts.

My passion for motorcycles was driving me to develop my own eye, my own sense of style and taste in motorcycles. Eventually, after going through the magazines, I'd come up with a concept. Not a concept for an entire bike, but just bits and pieces that I wanted to build a bike around. I would find a set of handlebars I liked, or a gas tank, or a rear fender, and then I'd apply it to the bike that I was building in my head. That's how I began customizing and— eventually—designing bikes.

Just a Hobby

I started working on bikes by modifying my own bike. In 1974, I bought a brand-new 1974 Harley-Davidson Superglide. This was when AMF, the bowling and sporting goods company, owned Harley. It was probably the darkest period in the company's history, when they turned out some of their worst and most unreliable products. But because I had passion, over time, I took that drab, AMF-era Harley road hog and, as my son Paulie likes to say, turned it into "a sparkling cherry-red customized old-school two-wheeler with handsome flame work on the tank (featuring a smiling sun) and back fender, and shiny retro wheels." I called it my Sunshine Bike, and I still own it today.

This point in my life was all about experimenting with what I could do with bikes, and how changing a few parts could make a bike look completely different. I was playing with the lines a lot and trying to find a look and feel that seemed right to me. I would cut the fenders into different shapes, which nobody did back then. Or I'd change the handlebars, or put different wheels on it. I'd experiment with all sorts of odds and ends and also try to incorporate some technology into the bikes.

Basically, I was fueling and nurturing my passion and growing my knowledge. Of course, everything didn't always work out for the better. Your passion can sometimes get you into trouble. But what is it that they say? "If you don't fail a few times, you're not trying hard enough." I'm a definite believer in that.

Knocking over the Table

I was working in my basement one day and decided to strip my '74 Harley down to the frame. Yes, you can customize your bike by adding a piece here and a piece there, but I wanted to start from scratch. I wanted to build a bike from the frame up. So I took my bike apart, took every part off, until there was nothing but the frame.

I had a Great Dane, Jason, and he got loose and went down in the basement and tipped over the workbench where I had the dozens of motorcycle parts laid out. I had laid them out in some order, so that I could put them back together again. Well, Jason upset all of that. The parts were scattered all over my basement floor. I had no choice but to figure out how they all went back together.

Some people would look at this accident as a huge obstacle. But for me, it was a great learning experience. That's because I had to figure out how all those pieces went back together and where they went on the bike. While that was a great challenge for me, I learned how everything fits together on a bike. More importantly, it forced me to pay attention to and understand a lot of the smaller parts that I would have ignored. Now I know every single part of a bike. And I not only know where each piece fits on a bike, but I know what it does, why it does it, and how it integrates with the other parts on the bike.

The same lesson applies to your business, no matter what it is. You have to learn everything about it, inside and out, and continue to learn as your business changes. If you have passion for what you do, it will not only compel you to do this, but make it a joy instead of a chore. And when you know every aspect of your business, it puts you in a position of power. No one can bullshit you about your business, because you know every aspect of it. So if a contractor comes in and says it'll take him 10 hours to do a job, but you know—from experience—that it can be done right in five, then you just saved yourself from getting ripped off.

So if you're looking to take your business to the next level, or increase your knowledge of how it works, my advice is to tear into the stuff that you know nothing about. Knock over a table and see if you can pick up the pieces and put them all back together again. It will be frustrating at times, but you'll be better off for it.

Having passion for your business is also what keeps you going when times are tough. And over time, passion will infuse every aspect of your business. It will not only drive you to be the best at what you do, but encourage the same from the people who work for you, even in far-removed fields like bookkeeping or shipping. It will define you, the people who work for you, and the way you do business.

For instance, if you're passionate about your business, you will welcome change. You will be passionate enough—and smart enough—to understand that there are always new ways of doing business, and your passion will drive you to embrace them if it means a better—not necessarily cheaper or faster—way of doing business.

Your passion will help you to stay organized and be efficient. Along the way, you will find new and innovative ways to operate your business. Your passion will lead you to hire good people. Hiring people who share your passion for the product you are making or the business that you are in will ensure they are dedicated to your business and seeing it succeed. They'll share your passion for doing the job right, every time, no matter how minor the task. Their passion will push them to never accept second best and take pride in everything they do, because it is all a reflection on them and the company.

Their passion will make you want to take care of your employees, because you appreciate people who share your drive, vision, and ambitions. You'll want to take care of these people, because you know that in our quick-buck world, people who share your passion and dedication to hard work are gold. You'll want to do everything you can to keep them satisfied and challenged.

Your passion and the drive for excellence that flows through your business will make your workers feel like family. In fact, sometimes it will inspire your kids, and they'll want to work with you because of the example you've set. Your passion will spread to them, and they'll understand that going to work doesn't have to be simply punching a clock. It can be about building something they can be proud of. Instead of merely meeting sales goals or putting in time, they'll realize that business can be about realizing your dreams and achieving your goals. This is, perhaps, the greatest gift you can give to your children and the greatest benefit of your passion for your work.

Your passion will drive you to succeed and never stop halfway. You'll never be compelled to cut corners or compromise to meet someone else's standards and ideals instead of your own. Your passion will never let you sell out. Your passion will also compel you to give back, because you'll realize how blessed you are to have found something that makes you get out of bed every day and strive to be your very best. Not everyone is lucky enough to have that. As a result, your passion will motivate you to give back to others.

Because of your passion to be the best at what you do, you'll learn from your mistakes. You won't see them as setbacks, but as opportunities to learn and grow and be better at what you do.

You'll learn to be humble, because that's what having to work toward achieving your dreams does to you. It makes you realize that you're in control and that you have choices. And the choice you make—every day—is to be the best that you can possibly be at the job that you love.

Most importantly, your passion will drive you to follow your dream. And that's what will make your business a success: the passion, drive, and desire to have a vision and see it through to completion. Even when your critics are telling you that it's impossible and you'll never succeed. For all these reasons, you must be passionate about what you do. Otherwise, you should find something else you *can* be passionate about.

4

Welcome Change

*W*hen I say "welcome change," that doesn't mean you have to sell out. And it doesn't mean that you have to stop halfway or compromise your goals. What it means is that you have to be able to adapt to changes that help you achieve your goals and dreams better, faster, and more efficiently. If you don't, you'll be left behind in terms of competing with others in your industry. To put it much more simply: You have to believe that an old dog can still learn new tricks.

You must also be willing—and able—to leave your comfort zone. Many businesspeople are simply satisfied with what they know and how they do things. They aren't willing to make any changes to get out of that comfort zone, which means that they are basically stuck at the level of success that they have achieved and may not be able to reach a higher level.

But if you're able to change your behavior and adopt new technologies, new methodologies and materials, and open your mind to new ways of thinking, you're much more likely to not only be successful, but to continue being successful.

I Don't *Have* a Fax Machine!

The simplest and most common example of adapting is introducing computers into your business. When my motorcycle business first started to grow, I didn't know anything about computers. And I didn't want to know anything about them. I felt the same about the fax machine. When customers and suppliers first started talking to me about faxing orders, I said, "I don't have a fax! I'll put it in the mail to you or you can come over and pick it up."

Today, Orange County Choppers not only uses computers to design, fabricate, and finish some of the parts that go onto our $150,000 one-of-a-kind custom bikes, but the old boss even has a cell phone and an e-mail address. Now that's progress!

It wasn't always that way. Like my bikes, I'm old school. Change doesn't come easy for me. But over time, because I have a passion for my business, I realized that there were better, smarter ways to do things. Some of this I learned on my own, some of it was brought into the business by my son, Paulie, and some of it was brought to us by the people we hired. Again, this is why you hire people who share your passion.

I make fun of myself and how resistant I am to change, but the truth is that I've always been pretty open to change; it just takes time to adjust. You have to prove to me that it is really a better way of doing business. But once I see that something makes sense, I'm all for it.

And as much as I like to think of myself as old school, I realize now that when I had my ironworking business, I was always looking for new and more efficient ways of doing things. When I first started working as a welder, basically the only thing welders did was stick weld. That meant: take the welding gun, put a welding stick in it that was used to lay your bead, and start welding. When the stick, which was about 12 or 14 inches long, ran out, the welder would have to stop, lift his welding helmet, put in a new stick, and start again. Using this process, it was very hard to get a straight, continuous bead. In fact, it was almost impossible.

Then the MIG welder was developed, which was wire-fed. This meant no more sticks. The wire was on a long spool and was fed through the end of the gun. At first it was difficult to get used to, and you really had to pay attention, but over time and with patience and determination, I learned that the MIG welder was definitely faster, more efficient, and more productive than stick welding.

When your industry adopts a new technology or advancement, and you're not familiar with it, you need to spend a lot of time learning about it and practicing it. This is another instance where your passion to be your best can benefit you. If you're just looking to keep the status quo, you think, "Oh hell, why do I need to learn this? I'm just fine doing it the old way."

But if you're motivated and driven by a passion for what you do, you look at a new piece of equipment or a new process with interest and excitement. It's just like it was when you started in your business: you want to know everything about this new piece of equipment and how it can help you be more successful. You want to tear it apart, get inside it, experiment with it, and learn all you can about it. You should approach advances or opportunities in your industry with the same fervor.

Know Everything About Your Business

I remember reading once about General George S. Patton. He was one of my favorite generals from World War II. He witnessed the power of the early tanks when he was in France during World War I. Being a great strategist and studying all he could about his passion— warfare—he immediately recognized the benefit of the tank. The tank changed the entire concept of the battlefield. Instead of being a static exchange, where two armies just stand across from each other in trenches and kill each other, the tank made the battlefield fluid. As a general, you were no longer limited by the mere movement of men.

But as much as Patton understood about the tactical and strategic advantages of the tank, he spent most of his time crawling around inside one. After a few months, he learned all there was to know about tanks. He was able to take one apart and reassemble it. He knew where every part went, what it did, and how it worked and integrated with the other parts of the tank.

You should do the same thing in your business. Know everything about it. And part of knowing everything about it is accepting smart changes. That requires keeping on top of your industry, knowing the latest trends and technology, talking to others in your field, and reading the latest publications. To be successful, you have to know your business inside and out at every moment. Know every part, how it works, and how it integrates with the other parts of your business.

When I first learned of the MIG welder, it was completely foreign to me. I was comfortable with what I knew about stick welding. I knew of the different metal alloys used in the sticks and what each was good for. Eventually, I became as good with the MIG welder as I had been with the stick. I've always been mechanically inclined like that and picked up things fairly quickly. And it's a good thing, because the MIG welder completely phased out the stick welder. If I hadn't adapted to that change, I would have been out of a job. It's that simple.

As far as productivity was concerned, the MIG welder had the stick beat hands down. There was an overhead trolley that followed you along. If you were welding a big superstructure, it would roll along with you, and you could weld plates and clips without stopping. It doubled my productivity. Adapting to change when it came to motorcycles was a little harder for me. It took more time.

Thanks to all those hours I spent looking at those stacks and stacks of motorcycle magazines I had in my hall closet, I not only learned what kind of bikes I liked, and what you could do to them, but I also learned what kind of bikes I *didn't* like and what you *couldn't* do to them. By studying the various models and styles of bikes, my tastes began to evolve. I actually started warming up to some of the bikes that I initially didn't think I liked. And it's a good thing when your tastes and style change slowly over time. It says that you're not only always learning, but you're thinking and evolving.

Sometimes when you're crawling around inside your business or industry, trying to figure out what you like and don't like, what works and what doesn't, it can seem like you're going down a lot of dead ends. Sometimes it seems like you're trying things that don't necessarily work for your business. But they're not dead ends, and they're not a waste of time. Because if you don't try them, then you don't know whether or not they work for your business. It's all part of the learning process you have to go through to grow or improve your business, no matter what business you're in.

If you are in manufacturing, there may be several ways to fabricate a part or package it and ship it. Initially, you may prefer using some methods and not like others. But over time, as you hone your business model, and it becomes more organized, more efficient, and—ultimately—more profitable, methods and processes that didn't make sense to you before may suddenly provide the solution you are looking for.

The same was true for me and motorcycles. As I've said, I always like the old-style bikes from the 1960s. They have a line to them—a flow—that has always appealed to me. And still does. But if the market changes—if consumer tastes change—you have to change with them. That's not compromising your ideals. That's not selling out. You're still going to build your product to your exact specifications and exacting standards you set for yourself. But you have to give your customers what they want.

Look at it this way: If Chevy painted all of their Corvettes purple with yellow polka dots, nobody would buy them. The Corvette's a great car—probably the best car you can buy for $70,000—but nobody's going to buy it with that paint job.

❧

Old Dog Learns New Tricks

So what is the difference between old- and new-style bikes? An older-style bike has a smaller tank, or what some people call a peanut-style gas tank. These tanks are much smaller than the tanks on the new-style bikes, which tend to be really big and flashy. The old-style bikes also typically have a sissy bar and either an upsweep exhaust or what they call a shotgun exhaust. These bikes are also kickers, which means the bikes have a kick start—no electric start on the old-school bike. The end result is a pretty clean-looking bike with not a lot on it: minimum parts, minimum wiring.

The new-style bikes are totally different. The whole drive train is different because they have very wide rear tires. That means you have to offset some things—the engine, transmission, maybe the front end—so that the whole bike is balanced. I first started to warm up to these new-style bikes in the mid-1990s. And it's sort of funny how it happened.

I rode down to Daytona for Biketoberfest with a bunch of guys, most of them much younger than me. They were all riding these new-style bikes, and I was on my old throwback. That's just me being me. Anyway, we get down there, and they start looking at some of these really high-end new-style bikes. They called these new-style bikes Pro Street Bikes. They've got some cash to throw around, so they buy a couple of them. On average, they paid about $40,000 each for these bikes. I couldn't believe it.

"You guys are nuts," I told 'em. "I could build one of those bikes for half that."

After they stopped laughing, they said they thought I was full of it. "You can build those old-style bikes, but you can't build anything like this," they told me.

Well, the last thing you want to do is tell me that I can't do something. Because I'll do it just to prove you wrong. I've always been a risk-taker. In my drinking days, I was the guy who would do almost anything on a dare. Once I got sober, I started applying that mentality in more positive ways. And if you're a risk-taker—not foolish, but willing to take a calculated gamble—you're more likely to be open-minded to new things. And that's the way it worked out for me.

Up until that point, I had been working exclusively with rigid-frame, old-school bikes. I only worked with frames from bikes built before 1984. That's because in 1985, while Harley-Davidson came out with the Softail, which had the more traditional rigid frame like the bikes of the past that I liked, it also had a rear suspension, with shock absorbers, which made for a more comfortable ride. To me, these bikes were the enemy. But I was going to prove these young jokers wrong. I was going to prove to them that I could build one of these new-style bikes and that it would be unlike anything they had ever seen.

So I quietly went down into my basement and started working. I started with a Softail frame and put a whole bunch of Arlen Ness parts on it. I had Paulie help me fabricate some parts, and he had some ideas of his own. Most Softails had struts on the outside, which, to me, broke up the line of the bike. By putting them inside, it made the bike look seamless and clean. We eventually called the bike True Blue, because of the pearl tone of the royal blue paint scheme we had chosen.

When my buddies saw what I had built, they couldn't believe their eyes. Mostly because they knew that I wasn't a fan of these new-style bikes. But I showed them—and myself—that I could adapt to the new tastes. And I could do it without sacrificing any of my creativity, standards, or quality.

More importantly, it marked a major change for me. As my son, Paulie, likes to say, it signified that I had joined the 1990s. I was no longer stuck in the Dark Ages of motorcycle design. I was no longer in my safe world of Panhead, Knucklehead, and Shovelhead motors from the days of old. I had not only embraced these new-style bikes, but I had put my own mark on them. Moreover, it was, I think, the first time that I really thought I could make a living doing this. It was the first time I thought I could achieve my dream—the one that had long been in the back of my head—that one day, one of my bikes would appear in one of the top biker magazines.

From Hobby to Business

Of course, this wasn't the only change I would have to embrace as I began to think that I could turn this hobby—this passion—into a successful business. One of the most dramatic and challenging changes was when I actually decided to retire from my welding business. That was a huge challenge for me. But I did it, leaving the day-to-day business to my sons, and retreating into my basement to relax and just focus on what was still just a hobby of building bikes.

That was 1998. I had been working 12- and 14-hour days for the past 20 years. I had gotten sober and drug-free, but I'd also lost my wife—she finally divorced me—and lost a lot of precious time with my family. But because I dragged my ass out of bed every morning, I had been a fairly successful businessperson. That welding business I had started with one truck and one welding unit had grown over the years. It had survived me and my two partners, Fred Gerini and John Grosso. It had grown from P&F Ironworks to Orange County Iron Works, or OCI. So I thought I deserved some time off.

Of course, I could never really retire. My idea of time off was to go down in my basement and start tinkering on my bikes. But for me, tinkering was 14 hours a day, drinking three or four pots of coffee, and never seeing the light of day. To me, it was heaven. I started by refurbishing my Sunshine bike, the '74 Superglide, for the umpteenth time. After I got that bike the way I wanted it, I built a custom bike for Paulie. All the time, gnawing at me in the back of my head, was the idea that I was actually making my dream of building bikes come true. That I could not only make a living doing this, but become one of the top custom bike shops in the country.

After all, I had proved that I could build a newer-style bike when I built True Blue. But at this point, it was still just a hobby in my basement. I was a long way from selling my first customized bike. I realized that to start a successful business, I'd have to truly accept— not just tolerate—these new bikes. I'd have to get into them, figure out what made them appealing, and then put my own unique stamp on them. Because just copying a trend doesn't work. You have to improve on what is already out there.

It was the challenge of changing to this whole new style of bike that motivated me. It was totally different from anything I'd done before. Moreover, I not only had to adapt to this new style, but I had to do it in a manner that blew people's minds. The bikes I designed and built had to be over the top—much more tricked out and unique than anything else that anyone else was building. When I was able to do that, I'd know I had something. That gave me the incentive and the confidence to know that if I could do this, then I would have something that could definitely be successful. It also meant I had to change my way of thinking and my vision of what a motorcycle is supposed to be. But over time, I not only understood it, but I pushed it in a whole new direction.

For instance, when the wide tires on the new-style bikes first became popular, the parts of the bike around those tires had to be made custom. Initially, before fabricators started making frames to accommodate these wider tires, no parts, or even frames, were available for these bikes. I actually cut my frames and widened the rear section of some bikes to adapt them to the wider tires.

I also had to weld gears and other parts together so that the front wheel, the engine, the transmission, the chain, and the rear wheel all lined up. That was a huge change. What drove the change? The way that it looked. It was different. It was unique and it was the beginning of the large-tire era. What did I think when I first saw it? Well, at that time, I had only seen it in a picture. I had not yet seen a wide-tire bike in person. But because I have an uncanny ability to visualize things and see things, I was able to make a wide-tire bike without actually ever seeing one. All I had to do was look at the picture and figure out from there how to build it.

I liked the challenge of having to do that, having to create it myself. While I wasn't really crazy about the wide-tire look, in terms of my business, I had to move in that direction. And that's where I am today. I'm not ashamed to admit that making the change was difficult for me. In fact, everyone in business, if they want to be successful, should be able—and willing—to admit their shortcomings. It's the only way you'll get better.

When it came to the new-style bikes, I simply didn't see the value in them. I felt like we were getting away from the feeling—the lines and the flow—of what a bike was for me. I said to myself (and anyone who'd listen): "What the hell are we doing here? Are we sticking with the tradition of the motorcycle, or are we going off the reservation?" I never wanted to merely copy the new style of bikes; I wanted to make them better, in my own way. I knew that would distinguish us from the crowd. And I think I was ultimately right. I think that's what made us a recognized brand right away.

We further distinguished ourselves a few years later when we started building theme bikes, like Spiderman and iRobot. They greatly enhanced our reputation because, like our early designs, these bikes were totally different from anything anyone else had ever done before. More importantly, it took the customized bike craze and put it in a perspective—in a genre—that every demographic could relate to it. You didn't have to simply be a motorcycle guy anymore. When people saw the Spiderman bike, whether or not they rode, there was an instant connection. That's what made us who we are, even today.

So long story short: If I hadn't adapted to that change from old-style to new-style bikes, I wouldn't be where I am today. In other words: Change or die. It's an old cliché, but it's true.

5

Building a
Reputation

$\mathcal{I}$f having passion is the most important element to creating a successful business, then leading by example and keeping your word, no matter the circumstances, is a very close second. Having passion is what's most important within your business. It's what makes you and your employees come into work every day, strive to be your best, and constantly challenge yourselves to be better.

But when it comes to relating to people outside of your business—suppliers, distributors, customers, and the general public—the example you set and keeping your word will be the foundation of your reputation. Adhering to these principles will tell people who you are, what you're about, and what your values are. And, frankly, if you don't have these two qualities, you might as well close up shop. Because word will quickly get out that you're not someone anyone else wants to do business with—and that's the end of that.

You'll also be an example to your employees, and that's important. Because by being an example to your employees, you'll encourage them to be examples to other people—inside and outside your business. Altogether, it's about building a stellar reputation both inside and outside your business—something that's invaluable and a key to being successful in business today.

I've Always Been an Example

Given how much you already know about my past and me, you'll probably laugh when I say that I think I've always set a good example. It's true. I may not have always set the best example in my personal life—what I did after (and sometimes during) work—but in terms of showing up, working hard, and doing the job right, I'd put myself up against anyone.

I guess I have my grandfather to thank for that. Although he saw me as nothing more than a workhorse, what I must have picked up is my ability to work hard and see a job through to completion. Even during my drinking days—from age 15 until I got sober at 35—I never missed a day of work. No matter what, I got up and went to work every day. I never missed a day of work because I was sick, hurt, or hung over. I'm proud of that. Regardless of what my shortcomings were, I was an example of a hardworking small-business owner. Not the best example. But I was an example.

By showing up for work every day, I was showing my guys—who also spent most of their evenings drinking—that there was no excuse for not showing up. I don't know if it helped any of them. I'd like to think that it did. But regardless, one of the most important things you can do in any business is to be an example to your employees. Once I got sober, I became an even more positive example for my employees. I also became an example for myself. I proved to myself that I could do it. I could make it happen. I could be a successful businessperson.

They saw that I not only had the confidence and dedication to run my own business and do it well, but also that my decisions and actions helped the business grow. They saw that I truly believed in the vision that I had for my business. They saw that I had the confidence to construct a building that was twice the size that I needed at the time. They were there when we not only outgrew that building, but added onto it and still had to rent space up the road.

I also set an example by clearing all of my drinking buddies out of the shop. It served as a major step for me, a message to my family, and an example to the people who knew me. It told them that I was serious about both staying sober and growing my business. Sure, it was hard at first. There was a part of me that felt like I was turning my back on them. But I knew that keeping them on in my business was not the kind of example I wanted to set. I didn't want the message to be that to come in and do just the bare minimum, or to come into work drunk, or to drink on the job was acceptable. So, as I like to say, I not only had to talk the talk, I had to walk the walk. I had to be an example.

Becoming a positive example at work and home was part of my lifelong goal to not let the expectations of others determine my destiny. I also led by example by taking on any challenges I faced at work. That's the way I've always been and how you need to be in order to succeed in business, especially during tough times. Even if you don't have a clue as to what you are doing, in business, you must figure it out and make it work. I've always been determined to learn whatever I had to in order to make my business a success. And by taking on any challenge, and conquering it, I not only built my own confidence, but I stood as a good example to my employees. I hope that by doing that I gave some of them the confidence to overcome their own shortcomings and doubts and achieve their own hopes and dreams. Because that's the greatest thing a boss can do for himself, his business, and his employees.

You must see yourself as a role model to your employees. People look to you, especially as the owner of a business, and to how you conduct yourself. For me, that means that I wouldn't ask anyone to do anything that I wouldn't do myself. People need to look up to you in that way and know that you're invested in what you're doing. You can't just walk around the shop, pointing fingers and barking orders.

This is especially true in a mature and successful business where, as the owner, you're mostly focused on managing the business. While that is—and should be—your number-one priority as the owner, it's also important to remind people that you once stood where they are standing.

Hands-On and Self-Taught

My experience in business has always been hands-on. Everything I learned was self-taught. And early on, I handled all aspects of my business. It is extremely valuable to know what all aspects of your business entail, then, even though your business grows and you are no longer aware of the smaller details, you will be able to oversee those parts of the business with an accurate and discerning eye. Neither employees nor vendors can lie to you and say, "This process or this job takes this long or costs that much." They can't mislead you, because at one time or another you did everything in your business.

That holds true today. Everything that we do in my business, I've done at one point. And I still like to get in the trenches and get dirty. I still like to cut and bend steel, bolt on parts, fix design flaws. I do it for two reasons: (1) it reminds my employees that I know everything— from the smallest detail to the grandest plans—about my business, and (2) sometimes an owner simply has to pitch in. It certainly should not be his primary focus, but from time to time, especially in a small business, you're simply overwhelmed with work—a good thing—and everyone has to pitch in to meet the demand.

Even if your business is in an industry that's never required you to work in various capacities to advance, you should do it anyway. For all the reasons I mentioned before: it'll make you a better business-person, a better manager, a better planner, and, ultimately, more profitable and more efficient.

Keep Your Word

One of the best ways to be an example—to your employees, your customers, and your community—is to be a person of your word. While you may be able to get away with breaking your word once or twice, if you repeatedly fail to follow through on commitments, disappoint employees or customers, or even miss occasional dead-lines, you will develop a reputation for being dishonest. If you make a commitment to someone, you'd better stand behind it. Because it really is true—in life and in business—that you're only as good as your word.

If you're going to commit to something, you have to see it through to completion, even if some factors involved are beyond your control. For example, if you promise to deliver a product to someone by the end of the month, and one of your suppliers says they can't meet the same deadline, it's up to you to make sure that they do—or to find someone who can. Because when you go to your customer and try to explain what happened, they're not going to hear a word that you're saying. Furthermore, they're not going to care what you're saying. They really don't care if one of your suppliers had a machine breakdown, had their factory burn to the ground, or one of the owners stole all the money and flew to Tahiti. All they're going to know and remember is that you promised to deliver something by a certain date, and you didn't keep your word. That's going to make them think twice about doing business with you again.

Your Employees Must Keep Their Word, Too

Keeping your word is not something that just *you* have to be committed to. It has to be an example—an inviolable work ethic—throughout your business. In other words, not only do you have to be committed to keeping your word, but everyone in your company has to, as well. All of your employees have to have the same mentality and the same commitment to goals and values, or there'll be a breakdown somewhere. I guarantee it.

Unfortunately, in the business world, this lesson is lost on a lot of people. When I was growing up, most people understood that your word is your bond. That means, if you say you're going to do something, you can be counted on to do it—in every aspect of your life. Often, this seems to not be the case anymore. Many businesses promise to deliver one thing, but only plan on delivering something less than that. Their promises are only to secure the initial business. Their philosophy is that once they get the business, they'll deal with the consequences of not following through all the way later. It didn't used to be like that. If you committed to something, come hell or high water, people could trust that you'd deliver, even if you had to work all night and all day to make it happen. And while that may not be a popular or very common ideal in today's culture, it's the way I've always done business.

Unfortunately, I had to learn this lesson the hard way. It took me a while to learn that not everyone has the same commitment to ideals and principles that I do and that some companies like to play a bait-and-switch game. Whether through their advertising or sales-manship, they promise you one thing, suck you in, and then fall short in the delivery.

I'm proud to say that I've never done business this way. I've always been a man of my word, and it has paid huge dividends. I guess I learned early on in my house, as a young kid, that if you don't do what you're supposed to do, you're going to get smacked. Fortunately, I was smart enough to learn that lesson early, and it transferred over to my life in business. I just figured that if you didn't do what you were supposed to do—show up for work, do a good job, do the job you said you were going to do—there'd be consequences. Harsh consequences. I didn't like those consequences, so I was always a good worker and—I think—a good boss.

This is one of the reasons why I've always had solid relationships with my suppliers, customers, and employees. I've always under-stood that you can't be hit or miss when it comes to completing a job and meeting deadlines. You have to get it done right and on time, and you have to do it every time. I can't stress this enough. If you don't do the job as agreed upon, the next time a job, or customer, or opportunity comes up, you'll be beat out by competitors who are more reliable. But if you do keep your word, and have a reputation for doing so, even if your prices are higher, customers will go with you because they know they can trust you.

Ask for More Than a Handshake

While I've always expected people to be true to their word, and for the longest time sealed deals with just a handshake, I got burned a lot of times. One of the first times I learned that people don't always keep their word in business was when Fred Gerini and I worked together at P&F Ironworks. We were taking jobs from Bill Belmonte. It took a while, but we eventually figured out that he was doing dishonest stuff behind our backs. He was taking a bigger percentage than he should have, not giving us the proper requirements for the job, and not telling us exactly how much material we'd need to do the jobs right. All of this was affecting our operations and our profits. Doing business with someone you can't trust is very risky and worrisome.

We decided it was best for us to do business on our own and parted ways with Bill. This way, we would have control over the jobs we bid on, the prices, the details, and so on. But, more importantly, we knew that we'd be making commitments that we could meet— no matter what. If everyone were like that, the business world would be a much better place. I wish it were, but it's not.

If I had a word of caution to business owners, it would be this: Even though you are intent on keeping your word and following through on your promises and commitments, don't assume that other people are, too. Unfortunately, that's not always the case.

In the iron business, I used to do a lot of work for contractors who would promise you payment by a certain date if you completed the job by a certain date. But what they often did was use the money they owed you, and spend it to pay off another project that they were behind on, and then tie you up in court. In the end, you'd be happy to get back 10 cents on the dollar.

Unfortunately, when your business is just starting out, you may be forced to do business with people like that. We'd all like to stick to our principles in every single circumstance, but that's not always possible. Especially when you're just getting started and need the work, or you simply don't know any better. But as your business grows and matures, you will have choices as to who you do business with. My advice is to get as far away from those who are less than honest as you can. Not only is it a headache to work with them, but it also reflects on you. If an honest vendor knows that you regularly do business with a dishonest one, they may be reluctant to do business with you, even if you've always delivered a job on time and on budget for them.

Your Reputation Is Priceless

It's like my mother used to say: "Show me your friends and I'll tell you who you are." Or, if you lie down with dogs, you'll get up with fleas. Pick your cliché. The bottom line is this: No amount of money is worth getting a bad reputation. So don't do business with these people, because eventually it will blow up on you.

Whenever you trust someone and they let you down, it's a shock to you. While it is devastating in personal relationships, it can be even more so when your business is involved Once it is done, nothing can change your feelings about the person. If somebody has turned on you, or done something that they shouldn't have done—ethically or morally—you can't go back. You can't erase it. And you just can't forgive it. It's a done deal.

In my eyes, if it's happened once, what's to prevent it from happening again? I think it's more of a hurtful situation than anything else. It's difficult to deal with. It's like losing your best friend. And I've had a number of situations—unfortunately—where I've been burned. It is, sadly, part of doing business and part of the learning curve you have to overcome to be a successful business-person, no matter what business you're in.

In the very beginning of the motorcycle business, I was dealing with a supplier who started sending me bad parts. I won't say who, because I don't do business with them anymore. More specifically, they sent me a set of shocks that was defective—twice. But who did the customer come to? He came to me, because I sold him a set of shocks that were defective. It didn't matter that they were defective when they came to me; it was ultimately a reflection on me and the products I was producing. And it could have been worse than that. The bad shocks destroyed the fender and almost caused an accident.

Unfortunately, the supplier did not stand behind their product. And I was their best customer. As a result, I sold someone a bike that was supposed to be a top-notch bike, and it failed. Now I had to take the bike back. Even though the supplier didn't keep his word, I had to keep mine.

Under the right circumstances, I would have continued to do work with the supplier. With defective parts or materials, it's often a problem that starts several steps back. It might start with the manufacturer, work its way down to the distributor and then to me, the buyer, and ultimately ends at the customer. You can't blame somebody for something they didn't know, especially if they take ownership for it. No one's perfect. Not even me. I understand that mistakes happen and that there are slipups. But that's not what happened here. They lied about it, didn't want to step up and take responsibility, and I eventually had to eat the cost of the defective shocks. I never did business with them again.

In a partnership, when a partner lets you down, you're in it a little deeper than you are with a supplier. It's not as easy to walk away from a partnership. You either bail out, or you try to work it out. Or you accept that that's the way it is for now. Even though John Grosso was a great worker and a great partner (for the most part), in his drinking days there were times when jobs wouldn't get done. It would put me in a position where I wouldn't be able to keep my word, because he wasn't able to hold up his end of the bargain. When you're dealing with customers, you can't bad-mouth your partner. If one partner is kind of going against everything that you represent, then it reflects on you. So that's another reason why I don't like partnerships.

With employees, it is a little different. You have to analyze each situation. For instance, even though an employee might let you down on a particular job, it might make sense to keep him around. In the iron business, if a guy is three-quarters of the way through a project, you can't let him go because he fails on one aspect of the project. Said another way: You can't cut off your nose to spite your face. You have to be smart about how you handle each situation and realize that sometimes it might be better in the short term to keep someone on than to simply fire him on the spot. It's not ideal, but it is what it is. Sometimes you have to eat crow, because getting rid of the employee will put you in a worse position than you are already in.

But you can't simply let employee failure go, either. You have to step back, analyze each situation, and decide what's the best path, both in the short term and the long term. In the short term, the best solution might be to keep an employee on, but in the long term, you have to make sure that it doesn't happen again. You can't allow an employee to consistently put you in a position where you're at risk of breaking your commitment to a customer. So you either have to fix the situation or get rid of the employee. It's that simple.

Sometimes—and this has been a hard lesson for me to learn—an employee's failure is my fault. I have high expectations and think everyone should meet them. Not everyone can. I have to understand and recognize that. Does it mean they're a bad employee? Absolutely not. It means that as a competent, smart, clear-thinking owner, I have to be careful to not give my employees more responsibility than they can handle at that point. That sets us both up to fail, and that's not a good thing.

Customers Can Let You Down

And, of course, customers can let you down as well. With customers who do not keep their word, you basically have to eat it—or at least salvage what you can. In the bike business. I've had customers who wanted us to build stupendous bikes for them, they're excited about it, and then I never hear from them again. I've also had commitments from customers who came into the iron shop, went over the details of a job, agreed to them, and then disappeared.

In the iron business, we used to cut railings, all lengths, all sizes, depending on the sizes needed. If a customer came in and ordered some railing and disappeared, then I had to look at my other jobs and see where I could best use that railing. It didn't always work out perfectly, but I always managed to salvage something. And it was better than the alternative, which was scrapping it and losing all the time, money, and material you had devoted to a project.

Be True to Yourself

While we all go into business to follow an interest and to make money, in order to be successful, it has to be about more than money. As a person, and as a businessperson, being honest has always been a part of who I am. That should be what keeps you honest. Not what other people think or the jobs you'll lose. Being honest is a reflection of your own self-worth. It says something about how you feel about yourself. So stay committed to your word—win, lose, or draw.

You'll be amazed at how much that commitment will help your business. Just as doing business with dishonest people may cause you to lose some customers and some jobs, being an honest business owner will draw good people to you. Once word gets out that you're true to your word, other honest businesses will want to do business with you. There will be a trust there that you will develop, and it pays huge dividends, both in the quality and the quantity of the work you get and the companies that want to associate with you. It's a win-win situation for everyone.

Perhaps the best example of me keeping my word and meeting my commitments was the time the paint-tank fire destroyed the P&F Ironworks shop. As I said in a previous chapter, I never missed a single deadline. I salvaged what I could, moved it into my basement, and delivered all of my work on time.

Another time, we were working on a high-rise project with 10 flights of stairs. I put all the stairs in, but once they were all in place, I realized that all the platforms were three inches too small. Looking at it initially, I thought it would be impossible to fix without completely tearing down the stairs. And if I did that, I would have never met the deadline.

Further complicating the problem was the fact that, at the time, my iron business didn't have a lot of expensive or fancy equipment. It was just my partner and me, and this was probably a 10-man job. But we thought about how we could do it and eventually came up with a solution. Without going into too much detail, I'll tell you that what we did was rig a series of cables and turnbuckles so that we could remove and fix one floor at a time without the whole thing collapsing. It was tough, required a lot of thinking and engineering, but it worked. The two of us worked around the clock, and we got it done on time.

More than simply showing our grit and determination, I think we made a favorable impression with the contractor. He knew we were smart, dedicated, and that, no matter what, we'd keep our word. And, again, it's all part of not wanting to fail. Or, to put a more positive spin on it, being determined to succeed. I absolutely wanted to succeed, and part of doing that was sticking to my word.

Honoring your commitments works for both your customers and employees. If you want respect from your employees, then you need to be true to your word. It'll also make them better employees. It will help them to embrace your business model, your corporate ethics and ideals, and ultimately your vision and passion for your business.

So what do you do if you can't keep your word? What if your supplier does have a fire or the treasurer runs off with the cash box? If you can't keep your word, there has to be some sort of legitimate reason for it. After all, things happen. And if you have always dealt fairly with a company, been a person of your word, and delivered the quality of work that they expect, most people will understand. But it should be the exception, not the rule. Remember, it takes a long time to build up a stock of goodwill, and you should protect it as best you can.

6

Stay Organized

$\mathcal{J}$t sounds simple, but some of the best advice I can give you about succeeding in business is to stay organized. It really is true that time is money. As difficult as it is to do, if you get and stay organized, you'll save a ton of time and, in turn, save a lot of money. It's that simple. No one ever taught me how to be organized. Like a lot of my business and work skills, organization was self-taught. I had to teach myself how to be organized, because there was no one else around to do it.

First of all, there was my home life, which you know about. Nobody taught me to be organized at home. I don't think anyone taught me to be organized in shop class in high school, either. They may have tried, but I wasn't paying attention. I first learned to be organized when I started working in steel shops, after the Merchant Marine.

∽◉∾

A Dirty Business

If you've ever been in a steel or ironworking shop—or in any type of manufacturing environment—they're usually a mess. In ironworking shops, you usually have to jump over piles of steel to get to workbenches and equipment. You often can't find tools and other supplies. There's basically junk lying all over the floor. And most steel shops are very dirty. After a few months of working this way, I realized that I did not want my shop to be run the way other shops I had worked in were. I told myself that when I eventually opened my own shop, I'd do it completely different. And I did.

I became organized mostly out of necessity. Early on in my welding career, I often worked by myself. Yet, I worked on jobs that would sometimes require two or three guys. So I had to figure out how to do it by myself. One solution, I quickly realized, was to stay organized. Because when you're by yourself or have only one other person to help you on a job, you have to compensate for that. You have to figure out how many different ways you can do something by yourself and still be effective.

You are somewhat limited in your creativity, because there are only so many ways you can do certain things. For instance, in ironworking, we work with a lot of 20-foot pipe. That's basically your raw material—the stuff you use to start every job. If you have no one to hold one end of a 20-foot pipe, you have to figure out how to do that and still cut the pipe, or bend it, or whatever you have to do to it. You have to ask yourself, "How am I going to compensate for the fact that there's just me, but this job requires two or three guys?"

That's what forces you to become organized, because in order to be effective when you're short of help, you have to be sure that everything—your tools, your materials, your plans—are all in a certain position. Otherwise, you'll be expending a lot of extra effort and you'll be counterproductive. While most people don't take the time to do this, by staying organized, keeping your workspace clean, and keeping focused, you'll be a lot more productive and, thus, your business will be a lot more profitable. In short, if you're going to be successful and build your own small business, you'll have to become adept at developing new ways to become more effective and efficient.

Early on, when your business is just starting out, you will probably have to explore and discover these innovations and time-saving processes. Hopefully, as your business grows, if you've hired the right employees, they'll start to do this on their own. But in the beginning, it will be mostly you looking for the faster, smarter, more efficient ways of doing things. It's also another way for you to learn more about your business and the best way to run it. It's all up to you. If you don't figure it out, no one else will.

And I don't care what business you're in. When a lot of small-business owners start out, it's just a one-person operation. Whether you're starting a dry-cleaning business, a Web design firm, or a small manufacturer, when you're first starting out, you're going to be short of time, money, and extra sets of hands. So you'd better figure it out. Not just for now, but for the future. As your business develops, you're going to have to figure out how to be productive and efficient, not just for yourself, but for your employees, as well.

And once you get the right employees in place, you'll have to encourage them to not only be organized, but to constantly look for newer, smarter, more efficient ways to do what they do. That's how you'll grow your business, expand into new areas, and increase your profits.

Be Organized and Efficient

It's also important to learn how to be organized and efficient, because you may have to apply what you've learned to another business or industry. I can tell you that I am applying all of the things that I learned about organization in the iron business to the motorcycle business. Without going through that learning process in the steel business, it would have been that much harder to get my motorcycle business up and running.

A lot of what goes into building bikes—especially the kind of custom bikes that we do—is fabrication. It is no different from the steel business. In fact, we even use a lot of the same raw materials: iron, steel, chrome. And we use a lot of the same tools: welders, cutters, computer-aided high-pressure molding machines. So everything that I learned about fabrication in the steel business, I'm applying to the motorcycle business. All of the processes and shortcuts I learned in the steel shop are coming back to me and helping me with my motorcycle business.

So thanks to this efficiency, I have a distinct advantage over my competition in the motorcycle business. That's because a lot of the guys in the motorcycle business have never worked in a steel shop. And because I worked by myself and had to rely on myself to think critically and solve problems, I have a knack for being able to figure out things.

Recently, I had to build a sissy bar to go on the back of a 40th anniversary Woodstock commemorative bike that we were building for Bethel Woods Center for the Arts, a new music venue built at the site of the original 1969 Woodstock music festival. That's the way it is around here. We're a small, but very productive shop. And from time to time, the boss has to pitch in to make sure that a job gets done right and on time.

So I took the dimensions of the sissy bar, drew it out on a table, and did all the fabrication with a torch instead of taking it to the water jet. I did it all by hand. How did I know to do that? Because I had made organization one of my core principles in the steel business. And what I learned there—because I learned it in an efficient, organized, productive manner—is applicable to my motorcycle business.

Know How Your Business Moves

It also helped that I've learned over the years how steel moves. As such, I know that there are certain ways of doing things with a torch. You have to know about how the steel is going to expand and contract as you heat it and cool it. Or, you have to know that if you're going to tack something—just give it a few quick hits of the torch to make it adhere to the metal—and then you want to move the piece, there's only a certain way to do that, too.

I know all of this because I know how steel moves. I know how it behaves. That's because in the early 1990s, I worked with an old German guy named Fritz—I don't remember his last name—who taught me about the properties of steel. He could heat certain areas of the metal, let them cool, heat them again, and shape them or move them the way he wanted. I learned a lot from him. And regardless of the business that you're in, you need to know how it moves, too. You need to know all the ins and outs, the quirks and characteristics. It's all part of the principle of knowing every aspect of your business so that you can be the best that you can be at it. No matter what it is.

Thanks to him and what he taught me about the properties of steel, I was able to work with a partner and build the longest truss ever assembled in the United States at the time. It was 120 feet long, and it was for a bridge-building project at Rockland State Hospital in Rockland County, New York, that we were hired to do. We made four of them. Because the trusses were being used for such a large span, there was very little margin for error. There could only be a one-inch difference between the height of the beams from one end to the other. A job like that requires incredibly precise work. And, more importantly, it requires you to know what steel will do when you heat it and when it cools.

My point is this: You can't be organized without knowledge. Knowledge about your business, the materials you work with, and the processes you use. And the more knowledge you have, the more organized you'll be, because you'll be able to anticipate what you will need and the best way to manage your needs. You'll be able to predict what will happen if you move a piece of equipment across a room or change the layout of your business. With that knowledge, you'll be able to be more efficient, more effective, and have a contingency plan for almost any situation. That's what will help your business to prosper and mature.

This is true no matter how big or small your business is—or how new or old. Whether you're working by yourself in a new business or expanding a 10-person operation to accommodate another five employees, you have to be able to set up your business to be the most effective that it can be. And if you've done that for yourself, then you will know how to do it with 10, 20, or 100 employees. You'll instinctively know the most effective way to organize tools and machinery, or a register and order forms, or even just your computer and printer, in your workplace.

Keep Your Employees Organized

This is also true for employees. When you're working closely with people and watching them work, you'll be able to teach them to work smarter, faster, and more efficiently. Over time, they'll mature in both skills and productivity. Before long, they'll be the ones showing you how to produce twice as much, in half the time, working half as hard.

Organizing your workspace will also force you to be more innovative. For instance, if you're building a 20-foot piece of wrought iron railing and your workbench is 10 feet long, how do you work efficiently and precisely with 10 feet of heavy wrought iron hanging over the edge? For me, because I've had to figure out problems like those in the past, I could do it quickly and easily. I'd have it set up, without building a whole other workbench, and do it all myself.

Having to devise new ways of doing things enables you to work faster and more efficiently when even greater problems arise. Once you start focusing on being more organized and, ultimately, more productive, you'll find that it starts to come naturally to you. You'll soon realize that time is money. And the quicker you get stuff done, the quicker you get paid.

A Commitment to Excellence

Being organized is also part of my commitment to excellence. It's part of my desire to be the best at what I do. In fact, I'm so obsessed with doing things the absolute smartest and most efficient way possible that I'm always thinking about new and better ways to streamline the shop. In the car. In the shower. Sometimes I'll lie awake at night and just think about how I can make my business better. Not worry, but think. There's a difference.

Planning your day and the tasks you need to accomplish ahead of time will also help with organization and productivity. I have a game plan every day when I walk in the door at work. I don't figure it out when I get there. I already know what I'm going to do, how I'm going to do it, and how long it's going to take me. If I have 20 people working with me on a project, I've already figured out what they're going to do, where they're going to work, and how it's all going to work out.

Being organized is also part of being a perfectionist, which is what I am. I firmly believe that you can tell what kind of a worker or leader someone is by the way they organize themselves.

Rick, the Perfectionist

At Orange County Choppers, we have a guy named Rick Petko who works for us. He's exactly like me when it comes to organizing his workspace. Everything is where it is supposed to be all the time. When you see someone who's organized, you know they've been around and have some experience. You know they have enough sense—or have learned through the years—that being well-organized is the most effective way to get work done.

It's also important to keep your workstation clean. Like I said, when I first started out in the iron business, the shops I worked in were filthy. And most of them are. It's a filthy, nasty business. But my shop has always been different. When you walked into my iron business, you could eat off the floor. I never allowed it to get dirty like other shops. To me, that was grounds for being fired—partly because it's unsafe, and partly because it's inefficient. I'm the same

way in my motorcycle shop. Everything is neat, clean, and organized. To do it any other way is simply counterproductive.

❧

My Sons Could Use Some Organization

If you watch the television show, you know that being disorganized
is one of my biggest pet peeves. In fact, this issue is one of the main
themes of the show. I'm constantly arguing with my sons about
being messy and disorganized. It really does drive me crazy.

While building a chopper, some of my guys often have tools and
materials scattered all over their workspace. Nothing is organized;
nothing is where it's supposed to be when they need it. It's extremely
counterproductive, especially in a mechanical environment. My son,
Paulie, can be disorganized when working on a bike. He leaves tools and
materials all over the place. When the tools and parts are scattered all
over, it negatively impacts other employees working on the bike. They
have to work around a mess when a project becomes disorganized.

Something else I've learned about people who aren't organized: If
they don't take care of their own tools and equipment, they're not
going to take care of yours. When I'm working with Rick or some of
the other guys, I want to know where all my tools are and that they're
where they're supposed to be. I don't mind people using my tools
when they need them, but they have to be returned to where they
belong. Rick is really a strong example of this. He takes care of his
equipment and workspace the same way that I do. And, like me, when
he borrows my tools, he tells me. He says, "I'm going to borrow your
torch." He uses it, makes sure it's in the same shape as when he got it,
and puts it back where it belongs. I really can't say enough about Rick's
organizational skills and how they help him complete his job.

I demand this of all my employees (except my sons, who I've
decided are hopeless on this subject). If you walk through my shop,
you'll see how meticulous my team is. They know where everything
is, why it's there, and where it belongs when they're done. Of course,

keeping organized is an ongoing battle, especially if you're in a growing business. If you're constantly expanding the workspace that you're in, or moving into a new space, it's a challenge to stay organized. I'm not saying that it can't be done. It can.

Unless, of course, you're talking about my son, Paulie. If you've watched the show, you know that we love each other. We simply can't work together. And the big rub for us is that he's disorganized. He simply can't work any other way, and it's a constant source of tension for us. About 90 percent of the time, that's what we're fighting about.

Teaching Organization

Of course, not everyone who works for me is organized when they first come to work for me. I won't fire a guy just because he isn't organized. If he is talented, I'll take the time to show him my way of doing things. That's how people improve in my shop. New hires have to get up to speed pretty quickly and impress me, understand why we do what we do, and be willing to change. Not everyone can do that, but if they are willing to try, they've got a chance with me. But if they don't get organized, then they're not productive and they're not working to their maximum capacity.

Looking back, I realize now that my organization skills really came in handy after the paint-tank fire destroyed my shop. After salvaging what I could and moving everything into my garage, I was able to wrap up the job I was working on because I was well-organized. I knew it was going to be tough not to fall behind on my backlog of other orders. The shop had been a good-size one, but the one-car garage was going to be a tight fit—if it fit at all.

That taught me that in order for my business to survive, no matter what the circumstances, I had to be very efficient in my use of space and how I organized my tools, supplies, and other work materials. Given the number of jobs I tackled in that shop, everything had to be positioned perfectly. I think that was when I really understood how important it is to be organized. It's when I first realized that if you want to be productive, and you're working by yourself, you have to figure out ways to get things done that would generally take two or three people to do.

To this day, that is how my shop is run, whether I'm working by myself or with 75 people. My shops have everything organized, stored in the right place, and in good working order. It's part of my work ethic. It's how I'm efficient and cost effective. Most importantly, it's how I'm profitable. And you have to be organized down to the smallest detail. As I mentioned, in the steel business, you're often working with 20-foot lengths of wrought iron. They have to be cut to size, according to the job that you're doing.

The system I eventually figured out for all of this was pretty efficient. I had my steel coming in one way. I stored my 20-foot lengths in one room, cut them in another, did the scrollwork in another. But it was all part of a system. And it was all laid out ahead of time, before I even touched a single piece of steel or iron. I knew exactly what I was going to do, how I was going to do it, and how much time it would take me. There's simply no other way to do it.

And you have to be constantly honing the system, thinking about how you can work smarter, faster, and more profitably. For instance, in the steel shop we used to make doors for horse barns. I've done thousands of them. When I first started doing them, I was able to do two or three a day. Then, as I refined and tweaked my production system, I was eventually making 50 a day. So, again, it's all in the way that you set yourself up.

∾⊙∾

Organization Leads to Growth

You also have to be organized if you're going to grow your business. This was especially true for me, because as my business grew, I knew that I'd have to be out of the shop more often. I was the public face of

Identification card from the Merchant Marine. It's amazing how much it really looks like Paulie. The Merchant Marine told me I had to include a middle name, which I didn't have, so I made one up: John.

The exterior of Orange County Iron Works was located in Rock Tavern, New York.

One of the Orange County Iron Works trucks parked just outside the shop.

Exterior work area at the Iron Works shop.

Cutting steel in one of the outside work areas at Orange County Iron Works.

Sunshine was my first Harley; it's a 1974 FX Superglide. It's called Sunshine because of the sunny paint job. I've changed this bike a dozen times over the years, but to this day, it's still my favorite. Incidentally, I have a tattoo of the sun featured on the gas tank.

Some of my bikes in my garage in Montgomery. And, of course, in the middle is Sunshine.

In my "workshop" in the basement of my apartment in Montgomery, New York, about 1997. This is what it looks like when you spend 18 hours a day without sunlight and live on four pots of coffee.

In the Montgomery apartment, working on one of the early bikes.

This yellow bike, with the nasty Viking guy on the tank, is the first rigid-frame bike that I built. It had a five-inch belt on it, which didn't do much back then.

That's me on True Blue, part of that first batch of straight-color bikes that I built in my basement in Montgomery. It was about to be loaded on the Iron Works trailer for my trip to the 1998 Daytona Bike Week.

I had these gas tank tins painted for my umpteenth reworking of the Sunshine bike. One side of the tank has me in a welder's helmet, pulling a portable welding unit behind my bike; the other shows Paulie pulling a crane.

These are some of the first bikes we built, sitting in our makeshift shop in the basement of Orange County Iron Works.

This is one of the first bikes that I built, and the first bike to grace a magazine cover, *American Iron*.

This is the first bike that Paulie and I built together in 1999 in the basement of the Iron Works.

These are some of the early bikes that we built in the basement of Orange County Iron Works.

This is the Spiderman bike on the lift at the Iron Works shop. It was the first theme bike that we built. Initially, Marvel Comics didn't like the idea of us building a Spidey theme bike, but once they saw it, they loved it. It wasn't featured on *American Chopper*, but this bike really put OCC on the map. The hip-hop artist, Wyclef Jean, now owns it.

That's me, sitting on one of our early creations, at our display at Daytona Bike Week in 2000.

This is the work area inside the first OCC shop at 10 Factory St. in Montgomery, New York—the main area where *American Chopper* was filmed.

The Jet Bike (on the lift) is the first bike we built on *American Chopper*, the pilot episode aired on September 29, 2002. The bike was modeled after a fighter jet and originally was intended to be entered into a design contest at Laconia Bike Week.

The Jet Bike was chosen to be featured on the cover of *American Iron* magazine. The photo shoot took place on the deck of the USS *Intrepid*, bringing the Jet Bike project full circle.

The POW/MIA Bike is one of my favorite bikes; it was built as a tribute to those whom we will never forget. I got the inspiration from a group of Vietnam veterans that I met at a motorcycle show in New York City in 2003, This bike represents America's enduring regard for those who did not return from the Vietnam War.

Little Red is one of my favorite bikes; it has the ape-hangar handle bars that I like so much, fat front forks, old-style spring seat, and twin exhaust.

The 10-Up is a classic example of a bad-ass old-school bike. From the impossible-to-see-over gas tank to the drooping handlebars, styling cues include an upsweep exhaust, hand fabricated gas tank and sissy bar, springer front end, and custom handle bars.

Orange Knucklehead is another classic old-school bike and part of my Old School series of bikes. This bike is a classic bobber with features such as a shortened rear fender, rigid frame, and knuckle-head motor.

The Greenie is part of my Sr. Old School series. The green gas tank and spring seat, along with the straight up handlebars, are classic old school.

The Orange Bobber is another bike in my Old School Series. The bike is true to the 1950s-style bike. I built it with Rick for an exhibit at Sturgis Bike Week in 2006.

The Pitchfork is another classic 1960s-style chopper with extended forks and elongated frame. I love the sissy bar on this, and how it contrasts with the simple, straight exhaust pipes. A great retro bike.

The David Mann bike was a posthumous tribute to the painter whose artwork was prominently featured in *Easyriders* magazine. This bike features custom artwork in Mann's style.

The Triumph Flames is another classic example of an old-school bobber. This bike was inspired by the first bike that I ever owned, a 1971 Triumph, which is still in my garage today.

I built this bike for a charity auction we did on the *Intrepid* in 2005 to benefit two organizations that support the military: the *Intrepid* Fallen Heroes Fund and the Fisher House Foundation. I liked the bike so much that I was determined to win it, and I did.

This bike was built for the television show *My Name Is Earl* and was auctioned off for the Make-A-Wish Foundation. Besides being a cool old-school build, Paulie, Mikey, and I got to be on an episode of *My Name is Earl* in 2008.

the company; I was the guy that these contractors and builders trusted. I was the face they wanted to see when it came time to bid a job.

So if I was going to expand my business, I knew I'd have to not only have the right people in place at the shop, but also the right system for work established: an efficient system that I knew would run smoothly even when I wasn't there. Without it, my steel business wouldn't have grown the way that it did.

As you may recall, early on in the steel business I was doing mostly residential work: railings for porches and other wrought-iron work for housing developers and contractors. But to develop my business, I had to diversify into the commercial building business. That not only meant that I would be away from the shop quite a bit, but as I expanded my business into new types of construction, I also had to come up with an efficient system to handle each one.

With almost every new job, every new endeavor, I had to regroup and figure out how we were going to accommodate this influx of new work. This was a turning point in my career. I had to start trusting my employees, especially when I wasn't there to watch them. This was always a hard thing for me. Not because I didn't think I had good employees, but because in my mind, the quality of the work—even someone else's work—was a direct reflection on me. That's just the way I was.

So I had to start depending on people, and one of the ways I could do that was by being organized. Having a system in place that I knew worked, that I knew could function without me, gave me the confidence to be able to leave the shop, bid new business, and know that things were being taken care of back at the shop. This was the time in my iron business when I went from about four employees to more than 70. When you're experiencing rapid expansion like that, being organized is very important.

There's an old saying: "You get paid for the car when you see the tail lights." Not when you're negotiating. Not when the customer is thinking about buying the car. But after they've actually bought it and handed you a check. The same is true for any business. Once you finish a product or close a sale and your product is out the door, then you can expect to be paid for it. If you have inventory sitting around your business, you're not making any money on it. It's that simple.

While money shouldn't be your primary motivation, you're in business to make money. And the quicker you sell your products, the sooner you get paid. When you realize this, the saying "time is money" is no longer just a cliché. It's a fact of life. Of course, so is hiring the right people.

7

Hire Good People

$\mathcal{F}$inding the right people is the most important step toward making your business grow and prosper. Finding these people, learning to trust these people with the most detailed inner workings of your business, and taking care of them if you want them to stick around are some of the most difficult tasks faced by small business owners.

I've long said—and I truly believe—that, "You're only as good as the people around you." If you don't surround yourself with good people, then you're pretty much sitting on the *Titanic*. Your employees can make or break you. In order for your business to be successful and thrive, you need your employees to do the same. In addition to hiring people who share your passion, goals, and work ethics, you also have to hire people who are smarter than you. And what I mean by that is smarter in areas of the business where you have limited expertise, such as payroll, benefits, shipping, and receiving. This is especially true in areas of management, where you give people control over important parts of your business.

My Own Kind of Boss

I learned about what kind of boss I wanted to be some 28 years ago when I first started working in the iron business. Over the years, I worked for a lot of bosses who were just plain jerks. They never gave you a compliment—or a raise. They never praised you for your work. In addition to promising myself that I would have a clean and organized shop when I opened my business one day, I also vowed to treat my employees a hell of a lot better than I had ever been treated. It's a philosophy that has paid huge dividends for me over the years.

I learned the principle of hiring good people before I hired a single person. I learned the importance of hiring good people while I was working by myself. These were the days when I did everything myself. I went to job sites and measured the railings, I cut the parts, I fabricated the railings, I painted them, and I installed them. When I wasn't working in the shop, I had to go out to sites to bid on new work.

As my ironworking business started to grow, I still did all of these things. Sure, I had employees, but I was still involved in almost every process of the job. I wanted to make sure that everything was done to my exact specifications and standards. As I've said before, even if someone else in my company was responsible for completing a job, I felt that if it turned out badly, or not exactly up to my standards, it was a direct reflection on me. I take ultimate responsibility for all the work that comes out of my shop.

There Is Such a Thing as Too Hands-On

While I still hold my employees to those same standards, what I eventually realized as my iron business really began to take off is that by still being involved in a lot of the production work, I was being counterproductive. I was spending so much time looking over my employees' shoulders that I wasn't being as effective as I could be in the area of the business where I was most valuable: finding new jobs and opportunities.

I eventually realized that I had to hire somebody who could carry part of the load. Someone who I could trust not only to keep an eye on the shop and make sure we were getting jobs done on time, but also to meet my standards. This person had to be not only trustworthy, but someone with the same focus, drive, values, and work ethic that I had.

Now here's the tough part. You can fully understand this concept. You can fully grasp that you need to be focusing on the bigger picture, while your employees and managers are taking care of the day-to-day operations. But understanding it is one thing; executing it is another, especially if you're a small-business owner.

Letting Go One Step at a Time

The best way to begin the process of letting go of some aspects of your business and entrusting them to another person is one step at a time. It's a long process, especially if you have high standards for both yourself and the people who work in your company. You may also go through a lot of people before you get to the people that you know are committed to your business plan, focus, and work ethics.

Here's the other thing: The people who ultimately don't work out are not bad people. They may be great workers and great people, but they're just not the right people. Or better yet, they're not the *perfect* people for the job. And as tough as it's going to be, you're going to have to find the perfect people for your senior manager positions. It simply won't work any other way. That's because of the high standards you have for yourself, your business, and your employees.

If you think back to Chapter 2, you can now understand better why I don't have partners. If you entered into partnerships with every manager you tried to hire, getting rid of them would be a nightmare. When they're just employees and it doesn't work out, it's a little easier. And, in my experience, the parting has been much easier, and I've often remained friends with a lot of my former employees. Again, they're not bad people, they were just the wrong people for the job.

If you keep this objective in mind, to hire not just a good person but also the *right* person, it will pay enormous dividends for you and your business. You'll be amazed at how it frees you to focus on other important aspects of your business. If you don't have to worry about day-to-day operations, then you can focus almost exclusively on the areas where you can be the most effective and generate the most work—and profits—for your company. With the right managers in place to oversee the day-to-day operations, it'll not only make your own business more organized, efficient, and productive, but it'll make you that much better as well. Because now you can focus instead on expanding your immediate business, planning for the future, and building a network of contacts with your suppliers, partners, and customers.

You'll Eventually Need a Management Team

Now what I've just talked about is hiring someone to oversee your day-to-day operations while you solicit new business and interact with suppliers, contractors, and customers. In my iron business, this meant hiring a foreman. In yours, it may mean hiring an assistant, supervisor, or department head. But as your business takes off from here, you'll need more than just an assistant to keep an eye on things. As your company gets bigger, you'll eventually need management. This is much different from a supervisor, department head, or foreman, because with a management team, you're actually giving them the power and authority to run major parts of your business.

You may get daily updates on the progress and performance of those divisions, but you're not going to be involved every day. The employees aren't going to see your face every day, and they're not going to see you walking around and checking on their work. In fact, depending on the size and operation of your company, your employees may rarely see you at all. That's because as your business develops, you have to have a management team in place that you trust enough to delegate some of your responsibilities for the day-to-day operations of the company. Now you're giving up some of your control, and you're depending on other people to run some parts of your business, as well as advise you on growing in the right direction, adding equipment or personnel, or seeking out new business opportunities.

Let me be perfectly honest with you: I got to where I am on sheer determination, confidence in what I wanted to accomplish, and a refusal to let anything stop me. I was willing to take a risk and succeeded almost exclusively on willpower; that is, my ability to persevere and not accept failure. That's okay until your business gets to a certain point. Both my ironworking business and my motor-cycle business had gotten to that point, so I needed people around me who could make good decisions for the company in areas where I wasn't necessarily an expert. Like I said, they're not necessarily smarter than I am in terms of the operation of the business— bending steel or building motorcycles—but they have certain specialized knowledge in areas that I do not.

You have to always hire people who share your passion, vision, and dedication. That's equally true of management. So, if I'm looking for someone to run my shipping department, I'm not necessarily going to hire someone who has an MBA in international affairs and a long list of credentials after his name. I'm more likely to hire a blue-collar guy like me, someone who's worked his way up, and gained a particular set of skills and knowledge that I don't have.

Protecting Me from Myself

Unfortunately, in this day and age, when everyone's all lawyered up (see Chapter 5), I also have to hire people who will protect me from myself. That's because a lot of my techniques are crude. Do I get the job done? Certainly. But it's not always by the most sophisticated methods.

As I told you, back in the early days of the iron business, I'd often get a job that came with certain conditions. Once those conditions were met—completion date, inspection, whatever—I was supposed to get paid. Unfortunately, not everyone out there is as honest as I am. So it would come time to get paid, and the contractor would dodge my calls, or say he'd send a check out tomorrow. Whatever.

Back in the day, I would only take this for so long. Eventually, I'd go down to the guy's office, walk in, kick his desk, and say, "Let's step outside and work this out." Unfortunately, I can't do that anymore (although I'd really like to sometimes). I have to admit, part of the problem was with me. Back then, I would do deals on a handshake. You and I work out the details of the job, settle on a price, shake on it, and our word is our bond. No contracts. No lawyers. While that may sound crazy today, it was a different time back then. My mistake was not realizing that everyone out there had the same business values that I did—including a commitment to being an example and a man of your word.

Today, I can't operate like that. Especially given the size and scope of my business. When I was in the ironworking business, most of my work was confined to Orange County and the surrounding area. Today, I'm shipping bikes around the world. I can't walk to Norway and kick some guy's desk because he hasn't paid me (although that would be a cool trip). Now, when a problem crops up, instead of me going down to the guy's office and threatening to rearrange his teeth, my people say, "Relax, we'll take care of it."

I think you get where I'm going with this. Now, given the size of my business, I have to have people around me to teach me a different way of doing business, a different approach. Again, this doesn't mean that you have to compromise your ethics or the way you do business. I hire these people to teach me a different way—a smarter, more efficient, more profitable way—to get to the same place I've always wanted to get to. Namely, turning out the most kick-ass bikes on the planet. The issue still gets resolved to my satisfaction. My people are just a little bit more sophisticated about it.

That's what I mean when I say that you have to surround yourself with people who are smarter than you in certain areas of the business. They have to have that same commitment to the end goal, which is perfection. And when we're in a crisis, they have to be able to stand on the front line with me and do whatever we have to do to make the business successful. I don't ever want to have to look back and see anyone in my management team behind me. They need to be willing to stand on the front lines beside me, not behind me.

While my management team today may have business skills that I'll never have, I still expect them to be as aggressive as I am. What I mean by aggressive is that there comes a time and a place for everything. And if the situation requires aggressiveness, I want my people to reach out and get someone's attention. I expect that. In other words, there's a time for finesse and a time for "Let's throw down." So, in essence, I want a staff that's going to fight for me.

You're the Face of Your Business

Being the public face of the company and negotiating all the deals can be an important role for a small-business owner. For you, it may require never leaving the business. You may *not* be the public face of the company. You may hire someone who shares your goals and values to do that for you. You may be the owner that the customer never sees until it's time to seal the deal. You may be the closer, the person they bring in at the 11th hour to work out the final details. That's up to you and how you see yourself best working within your own company. That may be out in the public or back in the shop. Whatever it is, you have to figure it out, hire good people to take care of the other parts of the business, and stay focused. It's that simple.

For me, it's always been about bringing in new business. And it may not be the same old business. My iron business really started to take off when I decided that we needed to expand beyond the residential work we were doing and move into commercial construction. And I felt that I was the one to do that. I met with the contractors and builders, hammered out the details of the job, agreed on a price, and brought the work back to the shop. If you're out doing that, you have to know that you have good people back at the shop who will be able to deliver the work on time, to the exact quality and standards that you expect.

For instance, I know nothing about accounting—at least not the kind of accounting my business required as it began to expand. So when you're hiring these people, you have to go on character. You have to make a value judgment right there in your office as to whether this person is going to fit in or not. Does he share my drive, my passion, and my determination? That's what you have to figure out.

❦

Think Outside the Box in Hiring

Sometimes you'll be surprised where you find these employees. A good example is a guy named Paul Peroni. I was his sponsor in AA. He was a car salesperson. His biggest challenge was his work environment. There's a lot of downtime to drink when you're sitting around a car dealership. And car dealers—like a lot of people—like to go out after work and knock back a few drinks. It was a very tempting environment for him. So he came to me and asked me for a job. I decided to give him a shot. I not only wanted to help him stay sober, but I had a good feeling about his character.

At the time I hired Paul Peroni, I was doing a job for General Motors. It required us to cut thousands of pieces of tubing. Dealing with tubing is one of the dirtiest jobs in the steel business, because the tubing is oiled so it doesn't rust. So I put Paul Peroni to work cutting tubing every day, 10 to 12 hours a day. At the end of the day, all you could see was his eyes. The rest of him was completely black, covered in soot. But that impressed me. It told me that he might not be knowledgeable about the business, but he was willing to do anything that he needed to do. Paul Peroni eventually became my shop foreman. I kept promoting him and giving him more responsibility, because he was willing to learn. Moreover, he was willing to learn to do things the way I expected them to be done. In other words, he shared my passion, my vision, and my determination to get the job done and to get it done right. Employees like that are pure gold.

So instead of bringing in someone off the street who already had experience in the steel business, I spent the time with Paul so that he could learn my methods. It was a huge investment on my part, but it paid huge dividends for me, my business, and for Paul. It was, as I said in the partnership chapter, a win-win situation. As my business grew, having Paul as foreman allowed me to do the things that I needed to do. I totally trusted him, and I knew he would get the work done, no matter what he had to do. Basically, he was a committed person just like me.

Eventually, I also put him in charge of hiring. Mainly because I knew he would have the same expectations of the people he was hiring that I would have if I were doing the hiring. I knew that when he hired employees, they would have the same work standards that we both had. And if they didn't, he would teach them just the way that I taught him. That was 20-plus years ago. Paul Peroni is still working in the iron shop under my son, Dan. So that really says something about a person's loyalty and how if you hire the right people, your business will prosper.

Of course, for all of this to work out, you have to not only be confident in your employees' abilities, but you also have to be able to trust them. That's harder still, as you'll learn in the next chapter.

8

Learn to Trust
Others

*L*earning to trust other people continues to be a very hard thing for me. As I said in the last chapter, when I first started out in the iron business, I did everything myself. I'd go to the job site and do all the measuring, then go back to the shop and cut the railings, paint them, take care of any fabrication that needed to be done, and install them. Even after I hired people, I still insisted on being involved in every aspect of the business, because it was difficult for me to trust people. I was also always very concerned about the job getting done right. As a result, I had a hard time trusting that other people would do the job correctly and to my standards, because their performance was not just representative of them, but was also a reflection on me.

But I eventually learned that there's only so much one person can do, and I had to let go of certain things if I wanted to expand the business. For me, trust has always been about walking the walk and not just talking the talk. In other words, I expect my employees, no matter what they do in the company, to lead by example. If they do that, then there's a chance they can eventually earn my trust.

Learning to Judge Talent

Judging talent is a wisdom that comes with time—and experience. After someone works for you for a while, you develop a general impression of that person and a sense of his or her work ethic. Today, I'm able to do this fairly quickly. I'm a good judge of character. You have to be if you're going to succeed in business. You have to develop the ability to look at someone's resume, find the strong points, find the weak points, explore them both in an interview, and decide if this person is a good fit or not. You have to have equally good judgment when it comes to the people you do business with: suppliers, distributors, and wholesalers. If they're not loyal, trustworthy, responsible, or don't have a track record of meeting deadlines or otherwise keeping their word, then you should not be doing business with them.

But when it comes to issues of trust, it's most important to have the right people inside your business. To ensure that you do, you have to develop a sixth sense about people—an instinct that they're not only the right people for the job, but that they also have the capacity to grow along with your business. That's the only way you're going to put together a management team that you can trust with integral pieces of your business.

I can tell right away what kind of worker someone is going to be. But there's a difference between a good worker and someone you can trust. A huge difference. Gaining my trust has always been hard. I've become better at it over the years—more out of necessity than anything else—but it was hard for me to trust my business to anyone else, because I'm such a control freak. I eventually had to give up that old mantra: My way or the highway. It was just impractical and not a smart, efficient, or forward-thinking way to do business.

I also eventually learned that people don't necessarily have to do things the exact way that I would do them, but the end result has to be the same. Again, it's not about compromising your standards. It's about learning to trust that your employees really do have the same dedication, drive, and determination that you do. A tall order, I know. But without this important step, your business is just going to stay where it is. There's no potential for growth there.

◌～◌◌◌～◌

Why I Like Rick

An example I talked about in Chapter 6 about organization is Rick Petko, who has been with me for almost six years. Before he came to me, he did auto restorations: historic cars, street rods. His abilities clearly exceed some of my abilities in certain areas—by far. But more importantly, he never stops growing. He's always willing to learn new things, new ways of doing things, but never ways that compromise his standards. Rick has a passion for what he does. Bikes are his thing.

Rick and I have a lot in common. He's a perfectionist, just like me. More importantly, he understands that by being a perfectionist, he's going to make a better product. With him, there's only one way to do things, and that's the right way. As a result, I trust Rick implicitly, and I consider him an employee that I would readily hold up as an example to others. Like me, he's very particular about his workspace and his tools. Like me, he's mostly self-taught. And he's always thinking three steps ahead. I like that.

The one difference between Rick and me is that he works well with Paulie. He likes to bounce ideas off him. And he really values Paulie's input (which I do, as well; I just find it hard to deal with his sloppy workstation and laidback attitude). And, I have to say, they're a good team. Paulie's very creative with his mind, and Rick can make it happen with his hands. They work well together. And Rick's ability to get along with Paulie, despite some of his shortcomings, shows that Rick's a team player. Like me, he understands that he's not always the smartest one in the room, and that there may be a better way, a better process, or a better tool for getting the job done. As such, he's always growing.

Rick also learns from his mistakes. When he first came to work at Orange County Choppers, he was unfamiliar with some of the paints and powder coatings that we use. But he learned by watching other people. He understood that while some of the jobs require pure muscle, a lot of them require finesse. And he didn't make the same mistake twice.

Rick, in some ways, also understands me better than Paulie or some of the other guys. Rick understands that all my yelling is my way of saying that I really care. That with me, it's really about getting the job done right and doing it right the first time. Yelling may not be the best way for me to show that I care, and because I yell it may not always seem like I do care. But deep down inside, Rick knows that I really care about my business and my employees.

In short, Rick Petko is my kind of guy. A model employee. Someone I can trust. Of course, I had to go through a lot of people before I found Rick. And they all know the rules from day one. If you're a good employee, I'll not only keep you around, but your loyalty, hard work, and dedication will be rewarded. If you're not a good employee, then you're gone.

Why Ron Made It

One of those guys who made it is Ron Salsbury. He started working part-time for me at the steel shop when he was 17 years old. He'd spend half the day in school, and the rest of the day he worked with me as part of a vocational educational program. He's still with me today, running the motorcycle department at OCC. Through all those years, I've always respected him. That's because he's always been a loyal employee. A man of his word, with a solid work ethic. He has the same passion, intensity, and dedication that I do. As such he's gained my trust.

Here's one way he did that: In 1998, just before I left the ironworking business to tinker with bikes, Ron had a herniated disc in his back. He could barely move. The doctors told him he had to lie in bed and rest, and he was in a lot of pain. About that time, I had a big job that needed to be painted. Despite the extreme pain he was in, he got out of bed, came to work, and painted the railings. In between painting each piece, he'd lie on the floor and rest because he was in so much pain. Thankfully, he recovered. And working through some medical conditions may not be practical or the best idea. But he showed me that he was loyal and dedicated to my business. That was huge to me.

Ron's first stint with me lasted nine years. When the motorcycle business started to take off, he came back to work with me and has been with me for about six years at the bike shop. When he first came to the bike shop, there were only about seven employees. Now we have 70 plus. He saw the business grow from a small garage. Back then, all the bikes were kept in an old storage shed that wasn't even heated. Since then, we've grown to the point where we're in a new 100,000-square-foot building, and now I'm not sure that's big enough. He's also watched as we got into merchandising, the television show, and as we build our dealer franchise to handle our new line of production bikes.

Ron saw similar growth in the iron business. He saw it go from Paul's Welding to Orange County Ironworks. When he started working for me in high school, the shop had just a few machines. He saw it grow from mostly ornamental residential work to more complex, industrial structural work. He saw how competitive I had to be in bidding on these new jobs. Ron's also seen me be a hands-on guy. He was with me when I used to be on the job site every morning, working side-by-side with the guys, doing whatever was needed to get the job done. He knows I'm not a suit-and-tie owner. I was right there, at the job site, from sunup until sundown.

He's always seen me lead by example. He calls me a role model for that. I'm not sure I'm that, but I appreciate the compliment. Maybe a more accurate statement is when he first came to work for me. Paulie, who was friends with him, used to tell me about how Ron told all his friends that his boss "wasn't normal." He'd tell them how the job would start at 5 A.M., and I'd be right alongside them. Once I was working on a job in Brooklyn. I was trying to make up for a slow winter and took this job that was an hour and a half away, but paid well. We'd leave at 4 A.M. to get to the job site by 5 A.M. It would be so cold, we'd have to use a blowtorch to warm up the crane before we could start it. We'd get done in Brooklyn at 7 P.M., fight traffic all the way home, get back about 9 P.M., and go out the next morning at 4 A.M. All winter long. Five days a week.

Ron also understands my two pet peeves: not keeping the shop clean and not showing up to work on time. When the shop would get out of hand, I'd come out, scream at him and Paulie, and they'd spend the next two hours cleaning the railing shop. It would take them that long to get it the way I wanted. But Ron never quit. And because he never quit, I not only learned to trust him, but I also taught him. He started out doing some simple shearing of sheet metal parts and some painting. Eventually, I taught him how to weld. When he came to work at the bike business, he didn't know much about that either. So I taught him about bikes. Today, his title is vice president of operations, which is a fancy way to say he runs the motorcycle side of the business. And he does it damn well.

How I Almost Lost the Iron Business

It's because of employees like Ron Salsbury that I was able to think about walking away from the iron business after 28 years and pursue my passion: designing and building motorcycles. Unfortunately, when I finally allowed myself to leave the ironworking business and spend more time in my basement, I assumed that the business would take care of itself, thanks to the people I had left in charge. It didn't turn out that way.

The iron business started to fall apart. Not because of people like Ron Salsbury, but because of the management team I left in charge. I thought I could trust them to run the business the way I expected it to be run. They didn't. It started to fail. My mistake was that I trusted people with a lot of experience in different fields that were basically uncharted waters for me. It was hard for me to tell whether they were doing a good job or a bad job.

For instance, we got into some more sophisticated work, where I was trusting people to take a full set of architectural drawings and pull out the parts that we needed to bid on. Once the bid was done, they had to detail the pieces of steel we'd need for the job, so that the guys in the shop could fabricate the parts. If the people doing the bidding and drafting the parts make mistakes, they are huge mistakes. If the job isn't detailed correctly in the planning stages, and you're building a Home Depot warehouse store, and nothing fits because of errors in the detailing, it costs you tons of money.

Now, the lesson I could have taken away from this experience was to never trust anyone. That would have been a mistake. Because, again, over my 28 years in the iron business, I realized that I couldn't do everything. The mistake here was simply putting my trust in the wrong people. The people I thought were managing the business properly were failing. And because I wasn't so involved anymore, I let it get away from me.

Steve Tells It Like It Is

Fortunately, when I put my management team together for Orange County Choppers, I had a little better luck in getting the right people. Steve Moreau, the shop's general manager, is a guy I've known for a long time. He's from Montgomery, New York, was friends with Paulie, and used to hang around the gym where we lifted. By the time he was 21, he had his own trucking business, moving product for 1-800-MATTRESS. He had 25 guys working for him; it was a pretty impressive operation for a kid so young.

He knew about our bike business, but when he saw the television show, he thought it was an opportunity that was too good to pass up. And he shares a lot of my core business values. He understands that it's important to listen to other people. Even though you've done something before, there may be a better way to do it. And he believes in my philosophy that you can't just talk the talk, you've got to walk the walk. He understands that a guy can be passionate about coming to work for us, but that doesn't guarantee that he'll succeed.

He also understands my concern that things in the business are being done correctly. He understands that it's not about me being distrustful of people because I think they're bad people, but because I'm so concerned about how the job and the quality of the work will reflect on my business and me.

As the bike business has grown from a small shop into a multi-national operation, he's helped me to understand that there's no way I can figure out what an accountant can figure out. He also understands the vast complexities of this business we call Orange County Choppers. There's a father. Two sons. A slew of corporate partners. A television program. Plus the usual suppliers, distributors, and whole-salers, as well as the headaches that come with running any business.

He also understands that it's important for all employees to set a personal example, but it's even more important for them to be able to function as team members. More importantly, he knows that I don't just automatically write people off if there's trouble. If there's a guy who's not fitting into the business, then you don't just cut him loose. You sit down, talk about the situation, and try to help figure the whole thing out. If we can't, we let him go, but we give him a chance or two.

I trust Steve implicitly. If he tells me something, I accept it as the truth, even if I don't know anything about it. I trust his judgment, and I trust his business sense. He was the guy who was smart enough to spot Scott Amann, our legal affairs manager. He was doing some work for us on the side, and Steve was so impressed that he said, "We need to bring this guy in-house. He's a guy who could help us grow beyond where we are now."

Steve also protects me from what we like to call the tire-kickers. Because of the show's popularity, we get a lot of people who come in and claim they want to buy a bike. In reality, they just want to meet me. So he weeds out the tire-kickers. If someone's serious about buying a bike, and they want to meet me, we'll make that happen. But I'm not in every meeting we have around the shop.

We went through a series of bookkeepers and accountants. Steve was the one who helped me to finally understand that I had to give up some of that control. As diverse and financially complicated as our business was becoming, I simply couldn't be involved in everything. But Steve always had the same goal as me. Namely, hire the best person for that job, and a person that we could trust.

He also helped me find Michele Paolella, our public relations person. She'd worked at a big PR firm in New York. But, more importantly, being from New York, she had thick skin. We can be pretty rough and raunchy around the office, and we give it out to everyone. No one's exempt. He recognized that she could hold her own and survive in this environment. And she has not only survived, she has thrived, giving us an expertise in communications and public relations that we've never had before. She's a great addition to the team.

Steve has also dealt fairly well with my two sons. As Steve likes to say, "What's above me are three Teutuls." He learned that when I was frustrated with Michael one day and said, "Steve, I want you to be in charge of Michael. I can't do it anymore." Steve said, "Okay, he's fired." That's the kind of brutal honesty I get from Steve, and it's invaluable. Of course, I could never fire Michael, but Steve has the guts to tell me that's what I should do. That's invaluable in an employee, especially when they can tell you something you don't want to hear and you actually listen and learn from it.

Ultimately, Steve is the best right-hand man I could ask for. He understands me. He gets my moods, and he can help me work through them. More importantly, he knows that our number-one goal, no matter what the position, is to hire the best person we can get. We may not get the best person in the world, but they'd have to be close. The requirements here are different, too. At some big corporation, it's all about having an MBA and belonging to a certain club. Here, you have to have the ability to roll with the punches. The management team is about 28 people, so there's not a lot of room for error. But as many of you know—or should—in business, there's never much room for error. That's why you have to surround yourself with the best people you can find and learn to trust them. There's simply no other way.

9

Take Care of Your Employees

*O*nce you get the right people in the right positions in your business, it is important to take care of them if you want them to stay. Understanding this concept, applying it, and executing it were very hard for me, because of my general mistrust of people. I can't stress the importance of this principle enough. And when I say "take care of your employees," that doesn't simply mean paying them well. It means more than that.

You have to do the following: (1) give them credit where credit is due; (2) foster an open and rewarding work environment where they feel comfortable taking risks and trying new things (even when they work for an old-school hardhead like me); (3) make sure they understand that they have a valuable role in a thriving business; (4) make it clear to them that you appreciate all the work they do, and in return you, the owner, are committed to doing your best so that they have a place to work; and (5) finally, make them feel like they're part of a family, not just an employee.

My Employees Are Like Family

This last point, for me, is the most important. Being raised in a family where the opposite was true—where no one took care of anyone—it became an essential part of my business and my own family. Because of this approach, my employees have never just been employees to me. They have become part of a family. I take personal responsibility for making sure that, in a sense, they're taken care of. Because they have families, too. They have responsibilities. And they have dreams. As the owner, I feel like I have a responsibility to make sure that all their hard work not only continues to benefit the business, but benefits the employees as well.

This is the work environment I wanted to create when I decided to start my own business. Mainly because I knew what it was like to *not* be appreciated by a boss. I knew, from experience, that when employees aren't treated well, they never give 100 percent. And I wanted employees who, like me, gave 110 percent to every job they did.

In a way, it all comes down to forging partnerships. I hate to use that word, but that's really what successful employer-employee relationships are. The only way this arrangement works is if the relationship is beneficial to me and to them. If your employees feel that they are not happy in their positions—aren't treated well; aren't paid accordingly; aren't allowed to grow and learn—then neither employee nor employer will benefit. They're going to be unhappy. You're going to be unhappy. Again, it's like having a seat on the *Titanic*. Eventually, it's going to go down.

Money Is Important, But It Isn't Everything

Like other parts of your business, money isn't everything. But it's not nothing either, especially to the people who believe they have committed to making your business a success. I don't care what anyone says, but money inspires people. That's a fact. It's not what it's all about, but it's part of the equation.

In previous chapters, I said that it takes a long time to get the right employees in the right position. Well, sometimes it takes a long time for the employee to *become* the right person. Sometimes you have to be patient with people—something that's always been hard for me. But it's a judgment call. It's like trust. You have to size up the individual, and if you think he or she is worth the risk, you have to take that risk.

Sometimes It Pays to Give People a Chance

A good example in my business is a guy named Greg Stiles. He came to work for me on January 6, 1985. I know that because the next day I stopped drinking—forever. So he only saw me drink one day on the job. Ever since that day, I've been sober. Greg was a real hard worker, and he was grateful for what he had. He was dedicated, and he was trustworthy—no matter what. To me, it was worth it to invest some time in a guy like that.

There was just one problem: He was a drinker. In fact, it got to the point where it was so bad—on the job—that I had to make a decision. And the decision was that I had to tell him that he had to either get help for his drinking, or he couldn't work for me anymore. It was a tough decision—for both him and me. He loved his job, he was good at it, and he loved working for me.

Getting sober was hard for Greg, and I eventually had to fire him. But he wouldn't go away. He would come into the iron shop even though I wasn't paying him. I'd come in, and he'd be up on a ladder in the shop, fixing something. I had to tell him, "You can't do this anymore." Being fired by me absolutely devastated him. Like I said, he loved working for me. Moreover, I think he always knew that I'd take care of him. That he wasn't just an employee, but he was part of a family.

The thought of losing all that gave him the courage to go into rehab. I admired that, encouraged him, and made sure that he knew his job was open when he got out. To this day, I think he feels indebted to me. I think he attributes his sobriety to me. That's flattering, but if you've ever battled alcoholism, you know that the credit goes to Greg, not me. I was happy to support him, but he did the hard work.

Once he was sober, he was still the great worker he'd always been. But now, he was able to think clearly and critically. And that was huge. Now he could make better decisions—for himself and for the business. He was more reliable, and I was able to trust him with some responsibility. Why? Because I took care of him, but I didn't coddle him. I didn't keep him on when I shouldn't. But I saw him as more than just an employee. I saw him as family. And in my world, you always take care of family.

Eventually, Greg was promoted to foreman in charge of my entire outside operation. He ran the part of the business that put up buildings and did steel fabrication, welding, and construction outdoors. It was a big part of my iron business. He had a lot of responsibility, and I put a lot of trust in him.

Recognize Your Employees When They Do Well

Part of making employees feel valued is by giving credit where credit is due. That, like trust, was a hard thing for me. It's hard for me to give credit to other people. It's a weakness of mine. Fortunately, I was able to recognize it as a weakness and correct it.

The reason I had difficulty giving credit to people was because I had such high expectations for others and myself. It comes back to walking the walk and not just talking the talk. I expected employees to give 110 percent to my business, because that was what I asked of myself. What I had to realize—what I had to remember from my days of working for bad bosses—is that while I have high expectations for my employees, I do have to acknowledge them when they meet those expectations. Yes, I expected them to work hard. But I also had to learn to tell them when they're working hard and succeeding, and that I appreciate it. And a little recognition will make your employees continue to work hard for you.

It's still difficult for me to say, "You're doing a good job," because I have such high expectations. I expect good work and nothing less. It's kind of like when I was growing up. No one ever used the word "love" in my house. I never heard anyone in my house say "I love you" to anybody. I had to learn that with my family, with my kids.

It's the same thing at work. I had to learn to say, "You're doing a good job."

And while I understand how important it is, it still doesn't feel familiar to me. But I'm glad I recognized my shortcomings and, as hard as it is, take good care of my employees. I think it's important to treat my employees like family. But sometimes, you really do have family working for you. That, as you'll learn in the next chapter, has its own challenges.

10

All in the Family

ou have probably figured out by now that family is pretty important to me. Both my work family and my real family. While I always wanted my own business, once I had kids I wanted a family business. Not only is it special on a personal level, but many successful small businesses—restaurants, grocery stores, gas stations, high-tech start-ups—are family-owned. But a family business can also be a love-hate relationship. That's how it is with me. While you want to share your work—your passion—with your kids, often it's not *their* passion. That's hard for some parents to take.

Then there's the problem of family issues and work ethic. The problems at home often manifest themselves at work. It shouldn't be that way. Work should be work and home should be home. But in a family business, all those rules are ignored. And often, your kids not only don't have the same passion as you, but they don't have the same work ethic either. That's been our problem over the years. And a lot of it's my fault. I'm such a taskmaster, such a perfectionist, that it was my way or the highway when it came to the way things were done at work. That created a lot of problems between me and my kids, even at home. If you watch our show, *American Chopper*, you know what I'm talking about.

My kids started coming to the iron shop with me when they were very young. Initially, it was to just hang around and do small chores. Over the years, as they grew up, and began wanting things, I tried to make them work for it. It didn't always work that way. Some of it was them; some of it was me. Overall, I think it was a good thing that they came to work for me. Even though they only worked part-time until they got out of high school, having them around truly made it a family business. I'd like to think they gained a sense of pride in their work, a sense of responsibility. Mostly, though, they learned that you don't get anything in this world for free. That's an important lesson and one often learned by working at a family business.

Growing the Family Business

Many of you reading this may have your own family businesses. I don't care what people say about the Dow 30 or the Fortune 500, the family business is the backbone of America. Keeping them healthy is what keeps the economy healthy.

What makes running a family business different from running other small businesses is that, in a family business, the relationships at home determine the relationships at work. Put another way, in a family business, you can't separate personal from business. Any time there's an issue on the job, other family issues are going to get mixed up into the equation. All the old arguments, all the old beefs—regardless of whether or not they have to do with the work issue at hand—are going to come up.

A lot of people watch our show, *American Chopper*, on TLC. Then they meet me and they ask, "How much of that stuff is true? How much do you and your sons really fight? How much do you really yell at those guys?" Many people are surprised to learn that it's *all* true. It really is reality television. We're not acting. That's the way we are at work. That's the way we are at home. That's the way we are in life. We have different ideas, different ways of doing things. We have different ways of working. My sons like to stroll into the shop at 9 A.M. and work until I let them go home. I'm there at 6:30 A.M. sharp, seven days a week. Small differences, I know, but they can cause problems. Put those things together along with other issues that come up in a small, family-owned business, and you're bound to have trouble. Having said all that, there's nothing like a family business.

As a father, I saw my family business as a way to instill values and passion into my kids. You probably do, too. Sometimes it works;

sometimes it doesn't. That's because while I demand perfection, loyalty, and honesty from my workers, I can't demand it to the same degree from my kids. They're my kids. It's that simple. You can't treat your kids like you treat your other employees. You can try, but it has been my experience that it doesn't happen most of the time. Again, you have too much history, too much emotion, too many issues from outside the workplace that manifest themselves inside the workplace. You can try, and God bless you if you can treat your kids like just another employee. For me, it's never worked that way.

Maybe that's because when it comes right down to it, when it comes to my kids, I'm a softy. While it may appear sometimes that I'm being too hard on them, over the years, I think I've been too easy on them. Like any parent, all I've ever wanted for them is the best. I've wanted them to have the things that I didn't have—the things I could never have. I often gave it to them without really making them work for it. And that's my fault.

Regardless of what your home life is like and how well you get along with your kids, at work they're the exception to the rule. Since my kids were very little, I tried to instill certain values in them: hard work, commitment, honesty. But in a lot of instances, they were able to get away with a lot more than my other employees. And that was a bad thing.

Making Up for Lost Time

Of course, part of my desire to pass along my values and business smarts to my kids is to make up for the lack of interest my parents had in my future. My father and I had nothing in common, and we never had what I would call a relationship. So I wanted to make sure that I did not repeat that mistake with my sons and my daughter. And I made it pretty clear to them early on.

After they each had graduated high school, I took them aside, and I said to them, "You need to make a choice. The choice is go out and figure out what you want to do in life, or come to work for me and be part of the business." My three boys—Paulie, Dan, and Michael—decided to come work for me. My daughter worked for me for a while when she was in high school, but ultimately decided to go into nursing, a profession I greatly admire.

This wasn't the first time any of them had come to work for me. When the kids were teenagers, they wanted stuff. I mean big stuff: motorcycles, snowmobiles, four-wheelers. And while I always made good money—always provided for my family—I didn't want to just give them stuff. So while they didn't work for me full-time when they were younger, I did make them come to the shop on weekends, holidays, and summer vacations.

Furthermore, I saw having the kids working in the family business as something that benefited all of us. It was a chance to spend time with my kids and teach them something about life—something my dad never did. And it was a chance for them to learn that you don't just get stuff in life. You have to plan for it, work for it, and follow through with your commitments. Along the way, they learned how to paint, weld, and do grunt work. Anything that didn't involve heavy, complicated machinery. That was the plan anyway.

My Son Dan

As a kid, my middle son, Dan, worked for me on and off for years. He didn't have much natural mechanical ability. He had to learn everything. Unlike Paulie, who basically came to work thinking he already knew everything, Dan was willing to learn. And what he didn't know or someone couldn't teach him, he taught himself. He was basically self-taught, just like me. He had the drive and the willpower to learn and to make something of himself.

When Dan made a commitment, he stuck to it. When Paulie or Mikey made a commitment to me, I had to drag them out of bed to make them live up to their end of the deal. Classic father-son stuff. I think Dan learned to work hard and stick to his commitments because he's had to work hard for everything he's earned in life. Dan learned how to be more independent and, frankly, more responsible.

Dan also had a passion for what he was doing. He not only wanted to be in the iron business, but he wanted to prove himself, just like I did when I was young. He took the time and put in the effort to learn everything he could learn to put himself in a position of responsibility. He wanted to know everything about the business. When he started working for me when he was in high school, in the late 1980s, he went from painting beams and railings to working with the foreman in charge of our outside projects, which at the time was the biggest—and most important—part of the business. And he made this transition fairly quickly—about a year or so.

Dan eventually learned the outside trade as well as anyone and was working solely on the outside business by the time he was about 19. Dan eventually took over the whole steel business, which was a difficult undertaking at first.

Like me, he had the same passion for the business that I did, knew every aspect of the business, and knew who did not have the business's best interest in mind. As a result, no one could bullshit him. Thanks to him, the business is thriving today, one of the biggest and most successful steel operations in all of Orange County, New York.

My Son Paul

If there's a polar opposite to Dan on this planet it's my oldest son, Paulie. Quite honestly, he hasn't had to work for much in his life. Not because he's lazy, but because he seems to have a natural ability to do almost anything he wants to do. When Paulie played football, he was the best player on the team. When he ran track, he was the fastest guy on the team. When he was competitively weightlifting, he was always the best. It all came naturally to him.

Because things came so easily to him, Paulie never stuck with anything. He'd try out for a team, prove he was the best, and then quit. He's the perfect example of how having natural talent can be both a blessing and a curse. It's no different today in the motorcycle business. I had to spend years pouring over those motorcycle magazines, watching what other guys were doing, before I really had a sense of what I liked and didn't like when it came to motorcycles. For Paulie, like most everything else in his life, it just came naturally to him.

We also have completely different work ethics. I'm organized, on time, and a hard worker. He's unorganized, comes to the shop whenever he wants to, and often gets distracted on projects. Because of these differences, the two of us are always butting heads. Paulie has his own way—a better way, he thinks—of doing things. And I have mine. Our ways are about as opposite as they could be.

Further complicating our relationship is the fact that Paulie is the oldest son. I guess I've always expected the most out of him. And as much as we disagree and argue, in many ways we're very much alike. We're both bullheaded. We both think we know the best way, the smartest way, the most efficient way to do something. But because I'm neat and he's sloppy, because I plan everything out and he does everything by the seat of his pants, because I put my tools away and he doesn't, we're like two bulls in a china shop. We're not only going to destroy all the china in the place, we're going to get a few good licks in at each other before we both crash out different doors.

Hoping for a Change

My hope has always been that there would be a turning point in my work and family relationship with Paulie. I had hoped that after all these years, he would have learned some of my work ethics, as well as developed his own. To some degree, he has, but not how I would have liked him to have developed them. It goes back to having passion about your business. So much passion that you're willing to do everything from chief cook to bottle washer—willing to learn every aspect of the business, whatever it may be.

In the iron business, Paulie was in charge of the ornamental work at one point. I think that's where he developed a lot of the abilities that have made him a success in the motorcycle business. That was the segment of the iron business that he gravitated to, and that's the segment where he stayed. In the early days of the bike business, he had some great design ideas. He had a good eye, a creative mind. He could take a fender, cut it up, and do things to it that would make it look different than any other bike out there. That's a real talent.

Unfortunately, our two styles are so different that it's hard for us to work together. Fortunately, we've sort of reached a détente. He handles his part of the business, I handle the rest, and we peacefully coexist for the most part. But we still butt heads quite a bit. And I'm not sure how to fix that. Maybe the partial peace that we have now is as good as it's ever going to get, and we just have to accept that. I'm really not sure.

I know you didn't pick up this book to read about my uncertainty. So if I'm forced to give you advice about family business issues, it's this: Work it out. Work it out the best you can. But with family, it's going to be tough because, again, all of those issues that you have at home, from childhood, are going to bubble up at work.

An Eye for Design

I think the greatest benefit of having Paulie in the bike business is his ability to look at something I'm doing and suggest how to make it better. A design, a process, a fabrication method. Whatever we're doing. He can look at something and analyze it right away. And, for the most part, I'm willing to listen to him.

Where we run into trouble is when I make suggestions. I may not have the eye that he does, but I have years of experience. I know what will work and what won't. But he's always reluctant to take any suggestions I make as constructive criticism or simply a father trying to teach something to his son. He has to do it his way. I was exactly like that for a long time, until I learned that I'm not always the smartest guy in the room, and my way may not always be the best. This is a lesson everyone learns at some point, and he's going to have to learn that for himself.

One regret I have about the relationship that Paulie and I have at work is that I would not be comfortable passing on the business to him. Not today anyway. Dan was absolutely the right person to pass the iron business on to. He knows every aspect of the business, and he's passionate about it. Paulie's not like that. Maybe he will be one day. But as I've said several times throughout this book, if you don't know every aspect of your business—and you don't want to know it, which is the case with Paulie—then you're going to run into trouble eventually.

If you're going to hand down your family business, you can't pass it along to someone who doesn't exemplify the principles that I've laid out in this book. They have to have passion for the business, welcome change, set powerful examples, and stay organized. They have to be committed, arriving at work before and leaving after everyone else. They have to be totally focused on the business, not easily distracted by things outside of it. Furthermore, they need to have not only a vision for the business, but also the ability to effectively relay that vision to others. They have to be the complete package, an *exemplary* power of example.

❧

Lessons of a Family Business

If one of my sons has not embraced the family business, it's my youngest, Michael. That's not to say that he doesn't have interests that he's passionate about. He loves books and music, knows a lot about history, and is a huge fan of the Coen Brothers' movie, *The Big Lebowski*. While I don't want all my sons to be carbon copies of me in their work or in their life, I'd be lying if I said that Michael's lack of ambition and interest in the family business wasn't both confusing and distressing to me. And while he has other interests, I worry that he hasn't found his true passion in life yet and how to make a career out of it.

This is somewhat baffling to me, because when my kids were growing up, they watched me work my ass off all my life to be a good provider for them. Where they get their work ethic or their values, I haven't got a clue.

My kids had to deal with me when I was drinking and doing drugs. Paulie was about 10, Dan was about 8, and Mikey was about 7 when I got sober. At first, I felt that I was responsible for some of their issues and shortcomings. But I don't feel this way any longer. As far as I'm concerned, they're adults now. And if they have issues, they need to take responsibilities for their issues, just like I do. At some point, people have to accept responsibility for their own actions.

Advice for the Family Business Owner

So what are my recommendations for a family business owner? Don't overcompensate. I think I overcompensated with my kids, trying to give them the things that I never had. By doing that, they never really had to experience what it was like in the world. I never let them learn on their own that you had to work for things, and that nothing is ever handed to you in life. It all comes from hard work—and maybe a little luck.

I think a lot of it goes back to my own childhood. When my grandfather said, "Paul, let's go over to my house, I need you to dig a ditch," that's what I did. My friends could be calling me to come out and play, but I couldn't go with them. I had to go do what was expected of me. When I was done digging the ditch, I could go out and play, but not before.

When I became a parent, I didn't want my kids to experience what I had. Is that a blessing or a curse? It wound up being a curse. If you give your kids too much, they'll always expect something for nothing. Teach your kids to work and be responsible for themselves. Unfortunately, I didn't do that. If Paulie wanted a new four-wheeler and we agreed that he'd work seven Saturdays in the shop to work it off, I'd let him off with only coming in four Saturdays. I didn't hold them to the same standard that I did my other employees. And, frankly, I don't think you can hold family to the same standard. You simply can't. You make exceptions for family. It's that simple.

But you can teach family members that there are consequences for their actions. Part of the problem with having family at work is that you can't just fire them. You can yell at them, make them do extra work, or send them home. But eventually, they learn that they can take advantage of the situation and not have any consequences. If it's an employee, and they do the same thing, there are consequences. With family, not so much.

That was the mistake I made. I should have taught my kids at an early age that there are consequences. If you do that, they'll learn the lessons of responsibility. Above all else, teach your kids. Teach them everything you know, even if they don't want to learn it. And, hopefully, they'll learn what you taught them and pass it on to their kids. That's the key to a successful, multigenerational family business. I'm not so sure I've created that yet, but I'm still working on it.

Despite all of these struggles, a family business is a great thing. It has its frustrations, but it has its rewards, too. My kids would be reluctant to admit it at times, but I think they've learned a lot from me. I think they've enjoyed working with me. I think I've taught them something about life and how to succeed. And isn't that the goal of any family business?

11

Learn from Your Mistakes

$\mathcal{I}$ wrote this book because I hope you will learn some important lessons from my over 28 years in the ironworking business. I hope this book not only teaches you some good habits and ethics that will make your business a success, but will also help you avoid some of the pitfalls that have hindered me over the years.

While mistakes do always have a cost associated with them, you will always learn more from making mistakes and paying the consequences than you do from reading a book and not actually experiencing it for yourself. This is especially true when you're dealing with a financial situation that ends up costing you money.

◌⟋⊙⟍◌

One of My Biggest Mistakes

Imagine you were building a set of stairs in a commercial high-rise. You can read how *not* to do it, and it doesn't cost you anything. But if you're putting in the stairs and you make a mistake and then you have to fix it, that costs you money. And when it costs you money, the lesson is learned. You quickly realize—when it hits you in the wallet—that you don't want to make the same mistake twice. So, in essence, it's an education. A valuable learning experience.

Looking back on my years in the ironworking business, I made a lot of mistakes. I made mistakes in bidding jobs, dealing with suppliers, and hiring the wrong people. But without a doubt, one of the biggest mistakes I made was when I decided to build my first shop. It was about 1986. I had been sober just a year. I was thinking clearly, planning not just for tomorrow, but also for five or ten years from now. With my head clear, I suddenly realized that I had a second chance at life and I wasn't going to waste it.

But because I still thought I had to do everything myself, I decided that I was going to build the building by myself. That was probably the costliest mistake I've ever made. Like I said, I'd made a lot of mistakes early on in business, but they were mistakes that I could correct without huge consequences—financial or otherwise.

Putting up the building myself was a mistake because—frankly—I didn't know what I was doing. It was a project that was beyond anything I'd ever done before. But I was in a hurry. In fact, as soon as I bought the property for the new shop, I went out and erected a couple of steel beams. I put up an overhead crane, and I started working right then and there. When I wasn't working on getting jobs done, I worked on putting up the building around what was essentially a dirt floor that I was using for my shop. I didn't have any electricity or other utilities. I used portable generators to run my welding machines.

Because I was bullheaded and driven to succeed, I eventually managed to put the building up. It was a long, slow process, but I did it. The problem was, I had to do almost everything twice, because I didn't really know what I was doing. Sure, I'd worked on big building projects before, but I had never seen the construction of a building all the way through, from start to finish. Specifically, I didn't know about inspections and building codes. It didn't help that the local building inspector had it in for me. Or at least I thought he did. Every time I'd complete a part of the building, he'd come out, look at it, find a number of violations, and I'd have to do it all over again. Literally. He was a real hard-ass and never, ever cut me a break.

Often, I didn't have to fix things just once. For instance, he'd come out, inspect the floors, and he'd find something wrong with it. Something that wasn't up to code. So I'd do it over, he'd come out again, and he'd find something else that was wrong. And that's how it went. For years. In the end, it took me about 15 years to get my Certificate of Occupancy for that building. It was a nightmare. And, of course, it hurt my business. Not being able to complete my shop limited me in the things that I could do. It limited the type of equipment that I could put in my shop, so that limited the kinds of work I was able to do. In short, it was a mess.

The net result was that all of my future building projects were *not* done by me, but by people I hired who knew what they were doing. Again, they weren't necessarily smarter than me, but they knew more than me in a specific area. Yes, I continued to expand my shop myself, with my own people. But it also caused me to learn about something that I didn't know before, namely building codes. In other words, I learned from that very costly mistake.

Valuable Lessons

So what was the lesson of all this? Well, the immediate lesson was that you can't do everything yourself, for all the reasons we talked about in previous chapters. You need to surround yourself not only with good people, but also people who have knowledge and expertise in areas that you don't.

At the time, people tried to tell me that I couldn't put up my own shop. That I lacked the technical know-how and expertise to do it. But because I was bullheaded and still learning, I didn't listen to them. When you make a mistake on the job, you actually pay for it right then and there. That lesson is invaluable. It is, in my opinion, more valuable than going to business school.

I also learned that you should never bite off more than you can chew. This was a hard lesson for me to learn, because I was so driven to grow my business and make it the best that it could be. I would never turn down a job, even if I'd never done anything like it before. Again, I was hardheaded that way (and, in some ways, still am).

Of all the lessons I've learned in business over the years, not taking on more than you can handle at a given time was, perhaps, the most lasting. That's because taking on more than you can handle can cost you added money in overtime, result in subpar work, and cause you to miss deadlines. When you're first starting your business, it is natural to want to take on as many jobs, clients, or customers as you can to generate revenue. What I learned over time is that you should stick to what you know best. When you expand into areas too quickly, or when you're not qualified, you risk your reputation in the business community.

You should always be looking to grow, in both knowledge and skills. You should always be trying to expand the scope of your business. But the smart way to do it is to gain the knowledge and expertise first, and then go after the new business. I did it just the opposite. I bid on anything and everything that came along. If I didn't know how to do it, I told myself, I'd learn and get it done. And for the most part, I succeeded. I never missed deadlines or turned in less than top-quality work. But this method often cost me in other ways.

A Big Learning Curve

The biggest learning curve for me in the iron business was going from residential work—railing for front porches, other decorative ironwork—to commercial construction. The main difference is the size and scope of the project. When you're making railings for porches, you're basically working with 20-foot lengths of wrought iron. You cut it, shape it, and do any necessary fabrication work. It's fairly manageable. But when you get into commercial construction, you're working with materials—like steel beams—that weigh tons. Furthermore, one slipup could kill you or one of your employees.

Moving from residential to commercial ironwork was a huge learning curve for me. I eventually made it. And it was the right thing to do, especially considering that at the time the residential market was slowing down and the commercial construction market was booming. But you don't have to be in the iron or building business to understand that there's a huge difference between putting railings on porches and providing the structural steel, supports, and other infrastructure for a multistory commercial building. I just went about it the wrong way.

Of course, going from residential to commercial is an example of taking a big leap outside of my expertise at the time. But the smaller leaps can hurt your business as well. For instance, it can be something as simple as bidding on a job you've done hundreds of times before, but maybe requires you to work with a special kind of paint you've never dealt with before. Let's say that it's a government job that requires you to fabricate steel beams, something you're experienced at. That part of the job goes okay, but when you get to the paint, you're completely lost, because you're working with materials and standards that you've never dealt with before. You don't get in trouble simply by taking huge leaps into uncharted areas of your business. The small mistakes can kill you, too.

I can't reiterate enough how important it is to stay within your realm of expertise, both when you're first starting your business and as it grows. Maintaining a focus on your core business can have phenomenal results. A good way to look at it from the point of view of my iron business is like this: If you build stairs or railings, don't agree to build the porch, too. That's not your expertise. A lot of contractors will do that to increase revenue. Instead of bidding out each piece of a job, they'll bundle the contracts. In this instance, they'll say "we'll give you the railing business if you build the porch, too."

Don't make the mistake of agreeing to do something that you're not qualified to do. The temptation will be great, especially when you're just starting out. The smart thing to do if you know this is the way the project manager operates is to get qualified to build the porch first, then bid on the ironwork and ask about the porch. And don't try to do it yourself. Hire the people who have that experience you need, and incorporate them into your business.

Another Tough Lesson

Another tough lesson that I learned is not to put people in positions of trust when you don't trust them. This goes back to some of the things I discussed in the chapters on surrounding yourself with good people and taking care of your employees. You not only have to learn to trust employees, but you also have to be careful not to put them into positions that you know they can't handle. Doing this will set your employees up to fail.

Unfortunately, I found myself in a position like that in my iron-working business. It had been a slow winter. There wasn't much work, and I decided that I needed to do something big to make up the difference. So I took a job on a big commercial project in Brooklyn, more than an hour from Orange County. The job did pay a lot of money, but it cost me a lot more in the long run. I had to get up at 4 a.m. to get to the job site on time, and I often wouldn't get home before 10 p.m.

Because I was out of the office so much, I had to trust one of my assistants to do a lot of the office work that I normally handled myself, including some of the finances. It turned out to be a huge mistake. She not only wasn't paying the bills and payroll taxes like she was supposed to be, but she was also embezzling money. It caused a huge headache, got me into trouble with New York State for a while, and in the end cost me more than I made on the Brooklyn job. The two lessons I came away from this experience with were (1) if you don't trust someone, don't put them in a position of trust; and (2) there are some things you should never delegate to someone else, because they're simply too important.

Trust but Verify

While I learned a lot of good—and costly—lessons in the iron-working business, when I got into the bike business, there was still more to learn. One lesson I learned early on is to be sure that when people tell you they have an expertise in something, they really do. This goes back to the issues of trust—and why, frankly, it's so hard to earn my trust.

I had a guy working for me who supposedly knew what he was doing. Turns out he didn't. More importantly, when customers started complaining about some defects in our bikes, it wasn't this employee who suffered the consequences, but me. In short, it hurt my reputation. It hurt me because I sold them a defective product—something less than what I promised them. And when they came back to me with complaints, I had to make good on my promises and redo the work.

Basically, this employee was putting the oil lines on the bike engines backward. With the oil flowing in the wrong direction, it wasn't getting to the engine, causing huge problems. The engines were getting hot, breaking down, and sometimes blowing up. With a good motor costing about $7,000 back then, having to replace engines, when we were just starting out, cost us a significant amount of money. Furthermore, because the bikes were inoperable, I often had to go to where the customer was and fix the bikes. Sometimes I had to travel half a day or more to get to where the bike was to correct the mistake.

Lesson learned? Make sure that no matter how much you trust someone to do a job right, make sure that someone else is checking their work. We all make mistakes. We're human. So someone has to verify that a job is done right. Common sense, I know. But it's a shortcut that's very tempting when you're first starting out, you have a small crew, and you're trying to save money. Trust me, the damage to your reputation—especially for a new business—will cost you more than you'll ever save by cutting corners.

Today, at Orange County Choppers we have a thorough system of checks and balances in place. Again, it's not that I don't trust most of the people who work for me, but we all make mistakes. It all goes back to the theory that you're only as good as the people you have around you. And it also relates to the philosophy that you can't do everything by yourself.

The Upside of Making Mistakes

Up to this point, I've only talked about the negative consequences of making mistakes. Some positives can come out of your mistakes as well. This is especially true in a creative business like Orange County Choppers. When you're looking for something different, something that will distinguish your company from all the rest, you have to make a lot of mistakes to arrive at the right formula, design, or innovation. It's part of the creative process. Along the way, you also learn where your boundaries are. You learn that no matter how cool something may look, there may be reasons—physics, engineering, design—why you can't do it. You have to learn those limits by trial and error.

A good example of this trial-and-error process is the evolution of our fender design. When I first started out in the bike business, we used to put fenders on a rigid frame. We'd use struts and mount the fender directly to the frame, either by welding the fender or bolting it on. But we found that no matter how careful we were, the mounting process would always result in some sort of blemish to the paint. A nick. A scratch. Or if you were welding the fender to the struts, the paint would bubble up or blemish. We fixed this by welding a boss—a crossways piece of metal—to the fender before we painted it. Then we would attach the boss to the strut. This helped to protect the finish on the fender. Today, we're not bolting the strut directly to the fender, but to another piece. A small detail, I know, but it solved a big problem.

Of course, we had other failures too as we tried to push the envelope on the design of our bikes, melding the look and the mechanics of the popular new-style bikes with the retro designs that I've always loved so much. We ran into some geometric problems early on. The easiest way to explain this is to say that you can only stretch the front end of the bike so far. There comes a point where no matter how much you engineer the frame and other parts of the bike, you simply can't put the front wheel that far out in front of the frame. What happens is that the bike is off-balance. The front tire will wobble and, at high speeds, could even cause you to crash.

We actually ran into this problem when we built a bike for a customer early on in the business. No one manufactured the kind of frame we wanted to use, so we actually built one. We bought a stock frame, cut it, stretched it, and raked it out. The customer came to the shop, took the bike out for a test run, and the front wheel was flopping all over the place. At this point, the bike was already painted. So we had to redo the whole front end of the bike, which involved cutting, welding, and repainting the entire frame. We eventually fixed it to the customer's satisfaction, and he took delivery of the bike, but it was a hard lesson learned for us.

You have to know your limits, but you also have to know how far you can push your limits. You can only learn this by experimenting— and failing—a lot. But it's all part of the deep passion you have for your business, and that drive to know everything you can about your business, including how much you can innovate in certain areas.

Don't Go Cheap

Another lesson we learned early on in the bike business is that it doesn't pay to buy cheap parts. We tried. Like any new business, we were trying to save money, so we tried various vendors for our parts. Unfortunately, cheaper means lower quality and less reliable, so the bike always comes back. Ultimately, you learn that, in the long run, it costs you more money to use the cheap parts and replace them than if you'd gone with a quality part to start with.

One of the biggest problems we had early on was starters. The motors that we put on our bikes are big—2200cc, turning out about 135 horsepower. You need a good starter to crank over a motor that powerful. We were using after-market starters, and they kept burning out and we had to keep replacing them. Many times, our customers would be stranded away from their home, and we'd have to get to wherever they were and replace the part. Needless to say, a lot of them were not happy.

The biggest lesson I learned from all of this is that you don't want to pay to do the same thing twice. Furthermore, learn from your mistakes the first time. It's good to make mistakes once, but don't repeat your mistakes. One of the best ways to avoid making mistakes early on is to be humble. As I've learned, being humble means being able to admit that you're not always the smartest guy. Sometimes, that requires you to acknowledge that you were wrong. I spent a lot of my life being humbled by making mistakes and by people taking advantage of me.

And being wrong is inevitable. Again, we're all human. Eventually, especially in business, you wind up in a situation where you make mistakes. You have to recognize those mistakes—take ownership of them—and be modest enough to accept them. This was another hard lesson for me. I'm a very competitive person. I don't like to be wrong. But if you're going to learn from your mistakes and not repeat them, you have to embrace this fact. If you don't, then you're not really learning from your mistakes. The worst thing you can do is know that you made a mistake and try to argue that it wasn't your fault. It's stupid. By failing to recognize your mistake and learning from it, you gained nothing.

Again, this was tough for me to learn. That's because when you're headstrong, like I was, and you think your business should go in a certain direction or operate in a certain way, and you're not listening or paying attention to what's going on, you put yourself in a position where, in essence, you're more liable for the consequences because you're not willing to accept the fact that you are wrong.

This is especially true when it comes to your employees, it's about being a power of example. Even though you're the boss, it's important for you to admit when you make a mistake. If you don't, it will severely affect the relationships and the level of trust you have with your employees. Once that attitude starts spreading through a business, the next thing you know, no one is taking responsibility for their mistakes.

This is compounded when you have a complex, multifaceted business like the steel shop. A piece of wrought iron that's being prepared for a job starts out as a piece of raw material. As it makes its way through the production process, you cut it, mold it, bend it, and fabricate it. If it's cut wrong, and no one admits that it was their mistake, then it goes unchecked. It could get to the fabrication phase, and you have a flawed piece of material, and no one knows where it went wrong.

I can't stress this enough: It's important for you as an owner to take ownership and responsibility for what you've done. People who don't take ownership for their mistakes are simply passing the buck. They never grow from where they are. They essentially have an attitude of self-righteousness, and that will eventually destroy you and your business, because there's no room—or even desire—to learn. If you can't take ownership of what you've done, how do you learn anything from it? You don't.

Of course, I learned a lot about taking responsibility and being humble when I got sober. That's because when you're drinking, you're in denial. You're not living in reality. When you stop drinking, you realize that the world is different. I think that, at some point, you have to look at what you've done and recognize that it was wrong, and you need to make amends for it, which is really part of humility.

It takes a bigger man, I think, to admit that he's wrong. Anyone can cop out and not take ownership for what they've done. Furthermore, you have to recognize when someone's in denial and not willing to take responsibility for their mistakes. In short, you can only argue a point of fact with someone for so long. If they're not willing to see the error of their ways, then there's nothing more you can do for them.

As long as you made the effort to take ownership for what you've done wrong, it doesn't matter what the other person thinks or does. You can't take ownership for their mistakes, only they can. You can't change other people; you can only change yourself. One way you can do that is by learning from your mistakes and becoming a better, smarter business owner.

12

Giving Back

I believe that you can't keep it if you don't give it away. What do I mean by "it"? Money mostly. I truly feel blessed in the sense that I am in a position to give something back to my family, my employees, and charities and causes that I care about. Giving back has always been a very important part of my business and should be for you, too. Money's great, but it doesn't give you what you get when you help people who are truly in need. For me, it's a heartfelt thing.

Giving back has always been part of my business model. I don't know where I learned that. Maybe because no one ever gave me anything. Maybe it's part of me wanting to be a different kind of person than everyone expected me to be.

Even when there were lean years, I could always find something to give to charity. And it doesn't always have to be money. As business owners, we can give back our time or our product. We can also encourage—but never force—our employees to give back some of their time and expertise. If you hired good people as I've recommend, they'll not only be happy to do it, but will find it as rewarding as you do.

And I've always considered it giving back when I give someone a chance. If it works out and they become a valued employee, I certainly benefit. But I consider the act of giving them a chance when no one else will a way of giving back to those less fortunate than us. I've done this is a variety of ways over the years. I've hired people who were down on their luck or who simply needed a second chance. A lot of times, good people make life-altering mistakes. They're not bad people, they just need someone to believe in them again.

On a more personal level, I've also given back by hiring people who were trying to get sober. Again, I was fortunate enough to be able to get my act together after 20 years of hard drinking and partying. I figure that if I can help someone else along that road, it's a way of giving back.

Being able to give back and reach out to people who are less fortunate than us really is a gift. By "us," I mean me, my sons, and my staff at Orange County Choppers. And almost every time a charity organization reaches out to us, I see it not as an obligation or a chore, but as a chance to do something special for someone who has life a lot tougher than I do. I get an immense amount of satisfaction in being able to do that, and make sure to do it every chance I get.

Making Wishes Come True

I am proud of myself, my success in business, and the fame and recognition of Orange County Choppers. But the thing that I think I'm proudest of is the fact that Orange County Choppers is among the top most requested wishes by kids who are supported by the Make-A-Wish Foundation.

To people who know me—or see me on television—I sometimes come across as a real hard-ass. In reality, I'm just a big softy. I have a real soft spot for people who are down on their luck or truly in need. I don't say this to brag. In fact, I was reluctant to write about this. I don't think you should do charitable works for the publicity, but for the true unselfish goodness of the act. But because this book is supposed to be about important business principles, and I think giving back should be one of them, so I'll talk a bit about my charitable giving.

I enjoy working with the Make-A-Wish Foundation because they give hope and joy to kids with life threatening medical conditions. They're kids who may not have the opportunity to experience what everyone else experiences in life. They've come to our shop in Orange County by the busload. We built a bike for them, the Make-A-Wish bike. We've had parties at our shop and barbecues at my house. We've done pretty much anything that we could to make them feel special and make it a day that they will always remember.

These kids get to experience us. They get an opportunity to see or be with someone they admire, watch on TV, and look up to and to see all the bikes around the shop and how we build them. Agreeing to host these wish kids and give them a day that they'll never forget is a pretty serious responsibility. No matter what's going on at the shop, how far behind we are on a build, I'll take the time out to do whatever I have to for these kids.

At our 100,000-square-foot facility in Orange County, I can't go out into our retail store during the day, because people shopping there will mob me. But if I'm passing by the door between the shop and the store, and I see a person out there with a disability, I'll go out and say hello to them. And when I go out, I'm not out there for anyone else but them. Other people will come up to me and want to say hello or get an autograph, which is usually fine. But when I'm out there with a handicapped child or injured veteran, I try to focus on them and make it all about them.

Giving Back to Those Who Protect Us

I also think it's important to give back to the police officers, firefighters, and first responders who were involved in 9/11—and the military in general. I've always admired people who do certain jobs, and these groups are certainly at the top of the list. That's why I'm so proud of my daughter, even though she has nothing to do with Orange County Choppers. She's a nurse, and it takes a special breed of person to do that job.

These people lay their lives on the line every day for a country and a way of life that they deeply believe in. And, quite honestly, I think the rest of us sometimes take that for granted. I think we forget that, without these folks out there protecting us every day—at home and abroad—we wouldn't be able to lead the lives that we do. That's why I think it's so important to make giving back to these people an integral and regular part of your business. The rewards you'll reap are so much greater than what you would have made by investing that money back in the business.

Giving Back to Your Employees

In addition to giving back outside of your company, it's also important to give back within it. This can be through recognition, promotions, raises, or, in terms of our discussion here, giving to or getting involved with an employee's favorite charity or cause. It can also sometimes simply mean putting your employees ahead of yourself.

Like any small business owner, when I was first starting out, money was very tight. Some weeks, I wasn't sure if I was going to be able to make payroll. But if it ever came down to me or my employees, I always made sure that they got paid, even if it meant I went without a paycheck. When the money from a job I was waiting on eventually came in, then I'd pay myself. But I always took care of the employees first.

Given my personal history, I've always tried to do what I could to help out other people who are struggling with alcohol and drugs. Over the years, I've hired a lot of recovering alcoholics and drug addicts, and I would like to think that giving them a helping hand when no one else would do so helped them on their path to sobriety. I was fortunate enough to get sober. I hope that by being an example to others who are struggling with the same issues—by coming to work every day, staying sober, and being successful—I, in some ways, reached out to people and tried to help them get their lives straightened out.

It all comes back to values—having them and teaching them. By being a power of example, and sharing your knowledge, expertise, and life's lessons with others, you're giving back. By teaching someone a trade and giving them skills that will put food on their table, you're helping them take care of their family and helping them to succeed personally. It gives them the opportunity to make something of themselves.

How to Make Giving Back Personal

Of course, sometimes the path to sobriety isn't that easy. I was lucky in that once I decided to get sober, I did it and stayed sober. It's not like that for everyone. For instance, I had a guy—I don't want to mention his name—who worked for me for a lot of years. He was a good worker, mostly reliable, but he was an alcoholic. He had worked in other shops, was out of work, and down on his luck. He came to work for me—part-time at first, but I eventually hired him full-time. I hired him because he was probably the best guy in the business at what he did, but he had severe problems with alcohol.

I tried to help him get sober, and for a while it worked. But from time to time, he would fall off the wagon. He eventually went into rehab and sobered up, but he had a family he had to take care of, so while he was in rehab, I continued to pay his full salary so that his family wouldn't have to struggle more than they were. Furthermore, I made sure that while he was in rehab, he understood that his job was waiting for him.

When he finished rehab, he came back to work for me and turned out to be one of my best employees. Some people would look at that as an investment, and they'd be right. I invested some time and money in this guy, and it paid dividends for me down the road. But that wasn't what mattered. It was a side benefit, certainly. But what was most important to me was helping a guy who was struggling with some of the same demons I'd struggled with.

By connecting with a charity or a cause that you understand, and letting the people you're helping know that you understand exactly what they're going through, you can not only make the charitable work more personal for you, but also more meaningful for them.

Helping Our Newest Citizens (and Hardest Workers)

I've also been generous to people from other countries over the years. While immigration is a hot topic today, the truth is that people from all over the world have always had trouble coming to America and finding work. Some employers discriminated against them because of their nationality or how well they did—or didn't—speak English. Fortunately, I was in a business where I didn't have to care where people were from or how well they spoke English. My guys—native-born Americans or otherwise—didn't spend a lot of time interacting with the customers. So I was able to hire a lot of non-Americans and give them an opportunity to make something of themselves.

Were they good workers? Certainly. I don't hire anyone who isn't a hard worker or who doesn't know what they're doing. When I looked at these guys, I didn't see merely good workers who would get the job done and get it done right. That was a part of it. But what I really saw was a group of workers who were just trying to make a better life for themselves and their families. And they weren't afraid to work hard for it. To me, that's valuable. But it was also a way of giving back—of helping out someone less fortunate than me.

I always had a lot of workers who emigrated from other countries like Mexico work in my structural shop in the ironworking business. These were people who had families and had basically gotten a lot of experience working in factories in Mexico—many of them owned by U.S. companies. But they wanted something more for themselves and their families, so they came here to find work. I admired that. So I was more than happy to give them the ability to make more money and continue to better themselves.

Giving a Skill or Trade

Teaching is also a way of giving back. Whether you're teaching someone a trade, a work ethic, or how to run a major segment of your business, it's a way of giving back while making an investment. An investment that pays dividends—at least to me—beyond the financial. You have to look at it from the perspective that if you take the time to invest in somebody who is in need, and it pays off, then that person has gratitude. If they appreciate you for giving them a chance, then they're probably willing to go above and beyond what the average worker would be willing to do for you, because they recognize that you went above and beyond for them.

One guy named Amil who worked for me knew nothing about the steel business, but his company was going under and he needed a job. So I hired him and trained him the same way I had trained other people. He started out doing simple tasks, but his advancement was only limited by his own ambition. In the end, Amil turned out to be one of the most productive people I had working for me. He still works in the iron business with my son, Dan. He really liked doing ornamental work, gravitated toward that, became very good at it, and is now shop foreman over there. Again, did I see some financial benefit from his work? Certainly. But for me it was more than that. It was about giving a chance to a guy who at the time had none.

Giving Back to the Family

Then, of course, there's giving back to your family. As I've said, I was always a good provider. As I said in the chapter on running a family business, that was both a blessing and a curse as far as my boys were concerned. But without a doubt, the greatest satisfaction I've experienced from giving back to family members has to be my mom.

I call her "mom," because that's how I feel about her. But she's not my real mother. She's not my biological mom. If you watch our show, you know her as Grandma Teutul. Her real name is Helen Blachut. She and her husband lived up the street from my parents. They used to hang out together. She and my mom always used to joke that if either one of them died before the other, they'd marry each other's husbands so they wouldn't be lonely. Well, that happened. My mom died and Helen's husband died. And she eventually married my dad. She's the closest thing I've ever had to a real mother, and I love her more than I can say.

She also taught me some of the values that guide me today. She has simple philosophies when it comes to life: "Just be good. Don't do anything wrong, because it'll only just come back to hit you in the face. Do unto others. Don't be selfish. Don't do anything you'll be sorry for." Sage advice. And it's what I shoot for today. To keep my life and my formula for success and happiness as simple as Helen's.

She eventually outlived my dad, too. When he died, she didn't have anyone to take care of her financially or physically. So I stepped up. I was able to pay the bills and take care of the maintenance on her house until she was able to sell it. I do whatever I have to do to make her life comfortable today. That entails being able to give back, because I'm in a position where I can do so. Day-to-day needs aside, I wanted to do something special for Helen, and that meant doing something with the New York Yankees.

Even though she was born and raised in Pittsburgh, Helen has been a Yankees fan since she was nine years old. So when we built a Yankees-themed bike for Jorge Posada and his children's charity, we made sure Helen was on hand for the unveiling. Meeting Posada— her favorite player—and some of the other Yankees was one of the biggest thrills of her life. We also took her to a game, sat in the owner's box, and had a hell of a time.

Those are experiences that, frankly, due to my fame, I was able to give her. And I was so happy to be able to do it. Building bikes for charities and giving back is part of our core philosophy. It's how and why we do business. And we reap more rewards from these projects than the ones that pay us hundreds of thousands of dollars.

Helen's other love was her 1985 Cadillac deVille. To her, it's precious. She loves that car. So, a few years ago, I restored it to its original condition—repainted it, redid the interior. It's like a brand-new car. I do these things because they are the most meaningful to Helen. That's how we do all of our charity work. We do the things that most benefit the people we are trying to help, not the things that most benefit us or Orange County Choppers. The greatest benefit I get from all of this is the feeling that I was able to influence someone else and change their life. And there's a reward in that. It makes me feel good that I'm able to do that or to be a part of that.

Helping Cristin

As for the rest of my family, I think they've always benefited from my hard work. Despite my years of drinking and doing drugs, I've always been able to provide a good lifestyle for them.

This is especially true with my daughter, Cristin. I was able to contribute to her education and help her to become what she is today. I have a lot of respect for my daughter. For two reasons: (1) she decided what she wanted to do by herself, and that was to help people; and (2) she pretty much tried to do everything on her own. So, to me, she's a powerful example when it comes to giving back, especially when it comes to her work with terminally ill kids. That's a hard job to do every day. It wears on you. But like a lot of things, it has its own rewards—namely the satisfaction of having helped someone less fortunate than yourself.

I think these good works are not just a benefit of being successful, but almost an obligation. When you become financially successful, you're able to do the things that most people can't do. You can reach out to a broader group of people.

Giving Back to Our Military

The other group of very inspiring people that we've given back to as our fame has grown is the military. We started getting involved with the military pretty much from the very beginning of our television show. The first bike that we built on the show was an Air Force themed bike that looked like a jet. Since then, we've built a bike for just about every branch of the service. In late 2008, we were working on a B-2 bomber bike. We delivered it to Whiteman Air Force Base in Missouri, where the B-2s are headquartered.

We've also done a lot for the Marines and their annual Christmas Toys for Tots program. Since my days in the ironworking business, I've always had the guys I worked with contribute to the program. But our charity work has definitely stepped up as the bike business has grown. And, again, our main purpose with all of this is to give back to the people who actually lay their lives down for us. They give to us every day, even though we may not see it or recognize it. So it's a small thing for us to give to them a few days a year.

This goes for the firefighters, the police, and the medics who responded to Ground Zero on 9/11 as well. Paulie designed and built a firefighter bike in tribute to the heroes of 9/11. I designed and built a POW bike that was a tribute to all of our prisoners of war and veterans, but especially to the Vietnam veterans.

We've hosted charity auctions for the military over the years, as well as built commemorative bikes for most of the services and lent our bikes and ourselves to help with recruiting. To help the military, I also donated my own personal vehicle, a relatively new Ford Excursion. I had it all tricked out and donated it to the auction to raise money for two organizations that support those in the military and their families.

So what should you take away from this chapter on giving back? Obviously, there's a certain importance to money when you're in business. But there's also the greater—and, I feel, much more important—feeling of having an impact on people's lives. I've been fortunate in that I've had the opportunity to have an impact on people from all walks of life. I prefer to direct my efforts toward people in need. Being able to give back is the biggest reward of being successful. It rewards you in ways that profits or meeting production deadlines never could. So I strongly encourage you to make giving back an integral part of your business plan from the very beginning. You won't regret it.

13

Never Sell Out

What do I mean by "never sell out"? That means never go for the quick buck. Never settle for less than what you expect from yourself and your employees. And never go against your core values. That last part is especially important. Your core values have to be just that—they have to be inviolable. They have to be something that no matter what—no matter the money, no matter the short-term reward—you never abandon.

I'd like to think that over the last 12 chapters, I've given you a good set of guidelines by which to run your business. I've lived by them, and they've always done right by me. Have I ever compromised them? Certainly. But I never truly abandoned them. I had to make concessions from time to time, but I always came back to these core values.

Be Ready for Challenges

When you live your life or run your business by a set of core beliefs, they are always going to be challenged. That's because life is never perfect. There are always times when work is slow and you're tempted to take a job that you wouldn't otherwise consider. There are times when you're short of cash or short of time, and you consider using less-expensive materials or cutting a few corners. And while it may have some sort of short-term benefit, in the long run it's going to kill you and your business.

One of my core beliefs has been that I'm responsible for the people who work for me. They've made a commitment to me, but they also have commitments of their own: to pay their bills, take care of their families, and to grow in their skill and expertise. So I feel committed to them. That commitment to my employees has kept me from selling out over the years, because I felt that I would not only be selling myself out, but selling them out as well. That has kept me from taking the business in a direction that may have paid a short-term gain, but ultimately would have been against my best interests. I've always considered how decisions I have made would affect those around me.

You should never compromise your vision or your passion. As long as you're in business, those two motivating factors should be constant. They should never end. If you wake up one morning and they're not there, then you should be doing something else. It's that simple.

Don't Quit When Times Are Tough—or Good

Looking back on those times when my iron business was struggling, either because of poor decisions I made or because of the economy in general, I know I could have done things differently. When times were tough, I could have sold my business or my building and my property and made a lot of money—especially during the 1980s and '90s when real estate development was on the rise in the Orange County area. But I didn't think it was the right thing to do. I felt that I could still make the business work—that there was a challenge to hang in there. I still had the burning desire to not only get my business to where I thought it should be, but to try and make it better than it was. I had no desire to take the easy way out.

Another time I didn't sell out was when I was under a lot of pressure to join the iron and steelworkers union. While I see the benefits on both sides of that argument, joining a union would have put a lot of my workers out of their jobs. Why? Because the unions have their own people. If I had unionized and was the primary contractor on an industrial construction project, the ironworkers union would insist I hire workers from their labor force. That's giving up a level of control in my business that I'm not comfortable with. Yes, the unions have some good people and some good education programs. But I may not be able to find the exact person I'm looking for in their labor pool. And if I can't, and I'm restricted to hiring from that group, then my business suffers. It has been my experience that unions always want more from you than they're willing to give in return.

Never Lower Your Standards

Lowering your standards is another way of selling out. I'm not talking simply about the quality of your materials or the level of craftsmanship that you put into each product you make. It could be something as simple as the distributors, dealers, or employees you work with. You have to scrutinize these people as much as you do anything else in your business, because these people are often the only human faces that your customers will associate with your product. If a company or individual you hire doesn't represent your product the way that you expect them to, and the customers are disappointed or turned off, then that's ultimately a reflection on you, not them. If that happens, then in a way—a very harmful way—you've lowered your standards.

When Orange County Choppers first became popular, there was a company that used to buy our bikes and then resell them. They used to beat the snot out of the bikes. They'd let their preferred customers take the bikes on long test rides, or they'd let their employees ride the bikes. The bottom line was that by the time they had sold our bikes, the bikes would be pretty beat up—in terms of the engine and transmission and other mechanical components. When the customers finally got the bikes, it wouldn't be long before they would start having trouble.. And guess who they'd come back and complain to? You got it: Us. It didn't matter that they bought the bike from this other company. What mattered was the fact that it was a bike built by Orange County Choppers. If the motor blew, they'd say that OCC had defective motors.

Be True to Your Vision

On the other end of the business model, you're selling out if you lower your standards in terms of design. As you know, when I first started tinkering with bikes, my passion was for the older choppers. The trend at the time was for the newer-style bikes. Despite this, I still stuck with the style that I admired the most. I was true to the passion that originally got me into the business. And although I had to adapt that image somewhat to be a commercial success, I never really gave it up. I did it my way—making the changes that would keep the bikes looking contemporary, without losing the elements I felt were important.

Furthermore, by not selling out, by not doing what everyone else was doing, I created a niche market for myself. Did I adapt my design to appeal to a broader audience? Certainly. But that's not selling out; it's simply recognizing the realities of the market. Today, there is a huge demand for retro bikes. The look has come back strong, partly because of the old-school styling cues that we kept in our bikes. As such, the market has come to me. Why? Because I didn't sell out. I stayed true to my core business, my instincts, and my passion.

You also can't sell out in terms of the quality of the materials and equipment you use in your products or services. In the retro-bike business, a lot of after-market parts are used that are made overseas. The quality is not as good as what I demand for my bikes. You want the finished product to be known for its quality and reliability as well as its style. To do that, you need to buy parts that are more expensive and more reliable. Does it cost more up-front? Sure. But the benefits in the long run can't be tabulated, because they're simply too great.

Don't Be Afraid to Be Yourself

Another example of me not selling out is when it came to the television show. When they first approached us about doing *American Chopper*, I didn't even like to have my picture taken with a camera. They were asking me to allow a film crew to come into my shop and record—on camera—everything that we did. My first reaction was: What am I going to do to look good, sound good, and give a good impression to the public? I knew that we were going to be seen nationwide, by millions of people. So I thought, "Okay, do I lose weight, do I dress differently, do I change my mannerisms?" I thought about all of the things that I might want to do to appear to be something that I was not. That's when I realized that the best thing to do was to just be myself.

I think that's what ultimately made the show a success. People who watch the show know that we're genuine. People can sense that. And I think people respect you more when you are who you are, no matter what. By doing that, it makes you just like everybody else. Other people have the same problems that we do; they're just not broadcast on nationwide television. Their problems, for the most part, remain under wraps. But by putting ourselves out there, just as we are, people realized that we're just like them—and that it's okay to be like that.

Every family has issues like we do. Every family experiences the same things we do, in one way or another. They're not different. People don't look at me as a celebrity. They look at me as part of their family. And that's because they relate to who I am, because I'm honest about who I am.

The same thing is true in business. You gain respect from people when you are just who you are, no matter who that is. I've met successful business owners and billionaires who are fascinated by who I am and the way that I conduct myself. They have a certain perception of me based on my persona. They may think that's not real, but when they meet me in person, they realize it's totally real. People that you do business with can tell if you're genuine, and they respect you more if you are yourself.

People can also figure out if you're a phony. Oh sure, you may fool them for a while. But eventually, they'll figure it out. They'll understand that you're selling yourself out to impress other people. That you're putting on airs—pretending to be something that you're not—just to impress them. It's the same way in everyday life. People who are phony will often act one way, but you will eventually learn who they really are. They may fool some people for a short time, but not for long. It's like the people who go to church every week and pretend that they're very spiritual. When, in reality, they're not like that. They're just pretending to be like that. They're really someone else.

People who give a false image are selling out who they are. And in the world of business, that's very obvious. The age-old example is the used-car salesman. You know right away that he's more interested in making a sale than he is in selling you the kind of car you really want and need. And it's obvious from the minute he opens his mouth. Now, if the guy next to him is a salesman and he's being honest with you, then that's the guy I want to buy a car from.

Perseverance Will Get You through the Tough Times

Another way not to sell out is to have perseverance. For me, in my experience, perseverance is a big part of being successful in anything you do. And that's not just in business, but also in life. You need determination, because if you fold under pressure, or you don't have enough drive to push your way through a difficult situation, you're losing the battle. There's no such thing as getting knocked down and not getting back up. For me, never selling out means that if I have a passion for what I'm doing, then I stick to that passion. I persevere—through thick and thin. If you sell out, that says something about how genuine you are. If you're genuinely involved in what you're doing, and it means that much to you, then you'll keep at it.

Being yourself pays off in every aspect of life. And it tells you that you're not ashamed of who you are. Basically it's a form of self-worth, which relates to the confidence you need to be successful in business. Because if you don't believe in yourself, then you don't believe in anything. Put simply: No matter what the circumstances are, no matter what position you're in, always remain yourself. Don't try to be something you're not, stay true to your core values, and trust your instincts. In the end, the truer you are to yourself and what you believe in, the more success you will achieve.

14

Always Follow Your Dreams

$\mathcal{I}$t sounds simple enough: Follow your dreams. But you'd be surprised how many people set out to do just that and end up giving up somewhere short of their goal. They get caught up with family, friends, or work that they don't really like doing. But mostly, it's because they don't really believe in themselves or their vision. This is usually due to a lack of self-confidence, a lack of vision, or simple laziness. Everyone has ideas, hopes, and dreams, but all too often they don't take the necessary steps to make them come true. Before they know it, decades have gone by, and they think it's too late. That their life is over. Thankfully, that didn't happen to me. And it doesn't have to happen to you.

One simple principle should guide you through all of the choices, challenges, and goals you face: Always follow your dreams. That's what I've done most of my life. It hasn't always been a straight path, but it never is. There have been speed bumps, detours, and brick walls. Fortunately, I've been able to figure ways around the obstacles and detours, and I'm just hardheaded enough to smash through the brick walls—and you can, too.

I'm Not the Person Everyone Expected Me to Be

For the first 18 years of my life, I was pretty much a product of the environment I grew up in. I was who everyone else expected me to be: a kid from a broken home, without much ambition, and without much of a future. That all started to change—slowly—when I went into the Merchant Marine and really committed myself to something for the first time in my life. I pledged to myself—to no one else—that I was going to get through boot camp. To everyone's

amazement, I did. And you can get through your own boot camps—
your early years—if you commit to yourself to do it. All it takes is a
little determination, a lot of hard work, and staying focused on your
goals.

There's an old saying: "A journey of a thousand miles begins with
a single step." That was my first step toward transforming Paul
Teutul. It was the first time that I realized I could make my dreams
come true. That I didn't have to be that guy everyone said I was
going to be. It was when I started to follow my dreams.

Start with a Few Steps

I don't know what you have to do to change yourself—only you
know that. But my advice would be to figure out where you are,
where you want to be, and take those first few steps toward fulfilling
your dreams. And never look back. Never stop. Never quit.

For most of my life, I've been focused on two very specific goals:
(1) to be a successful businessperson, and (2) to have one of my
motorcycles featured in a biker magazine. I wanted to be a successful
businessperson to be my own boss and provide for my family, but I
also wanted to prove to the world that I wasn't going to be the failure
that everyone expected me to be. For the most part, I did that. More
importantly, I did it on my own—and you can, too.

I started out with nothing more than an old beat-up truck, one
welding unit, and a determination to never quit. The rest, I learned
along the way. After 28 years, I had one of the most successful
businesses in Orange County. Furthermore, I'd built a business and
a management team that I felt confident walking away from to
pursue my other dream: building motorcycles.

I rode my first motorcycle in the early 1970s. I was instantly
hooked. I knew right then and there that it was going to be my life's
passion: something that would never grow old, something that I
would never get tired of learning about. That's true today.

Motorcycles are my life's work, my joy, and my passion. You have to learn what your passion is, nurture it, and never let it go.

The real leap for me came in the late 1990s, shortly after we sold our first few bikes. I took $120,000 out of my retirement and savings, put it into the bike business, and never looked back. Today, Orange County Choppers is the most recognized brand in the specialty motorcycle business. We were a major influence and driving force in taking a niche product and making it popular in more than 160 countries. We did this through our hard work, our commitment to what we believed in, and our unrelenting focus on quality (it also didn't hurt that we had a television show, *American Chopper*). Today, OCC continues to grow in dealerships, distribution, licensing and merchandising, and a new line of production bikes.

No Such Thing as an Overnight Success

Of course, none of this happened overnight. It wasn't until the late 1990s that I felt I was able to pursue my passion for motorcycles. You, too, have to have patience with your dreams. Success is not something that happens overnight, and it's a constant challenge. You can never lose sight of that. You can never stop trying to make your business smarter, more efficient, and more profitable.

Following your dreams takes time and hard work. There are good times and bad. Times when you're flush and when you're broke. One day, you can feel like you've got your business exactly where you want it, producing the right product, with the right people, in the right facility. Then one of your best employees turns in their resignation, or the market shifts. You have to adapt, and do it quickly. If these challenges seem like a never-ending nightmare, then you're in the wrong business. But if you look at them as a challenge, to you and your business, then you're probably in the right place.

Believe in Yourself

If you believe in that journey and make it your daily goal, then your business will be a success. But it will also mean that you'll never sit back and accept things as they are; you'll never be done perfecting your business. You will learn and grow. You will discover new and innovative ways to make your business better. New technologies will come along that will help you work smarter and be more efficient. Again, perfecting your business will not be a goal with an endpoint, but a never-ending part of your daily routine.

As successful as Orange Country Choppers is today, I'm still thinking about what I want it to be five or ten years from now. I'm always looking for ways that I can not only improve my business, but expand it into new and dynamic areas that build on my success. You have to do the same thing. You must always be looking for ways to make your business better. Only then will it—and you—continue to grow.

A New Chapter for Us

One day, I realized that Orange County Choppers had this enormous visibility. The television show, *American Chopper*, on TLC is seen in 160 countries. OCC was no longer just a well-known custom motorcycle company; it had become a worldwide brand. In addition to our custom motorcycles, we were selling more merchandise and apparel than I'd ever thought possible. But because we were building every bike by hand and to order, I realized that a lot of people wanted an Orange County Chopper but couldn't have one for two reasons: (1) they didn't have the money to buy one, and   (2) we didn't have the time, space, or personnel to build one for everyone who did want to buy one.

While all this was great, I realized that we have hundreds of thousands of fans, around the world, but not everyone could afford a $150,000 customized chopper. So I started thinking about a production line of bikes. They'll cost somewhere between $30,000 and $50,000. They'll have many of the same design and styling cues as the custom bikes we make. And, of course, the craftsmanship will be the same. The only difference really is that they'll be affordable for the Average Joe—and I like that.

So in early 2007, I decided that it was a good time to start a line of OCC production bikes. It's the newest phase of the business and will take the brand to a whole new level. And while you may be successful at what you're doing, you have to constantly be on the lookout for the next phase of your business. What's the next area that you can move into that will expand your business in a positive direction?

Making production bikes wasn't the plan when I started working in my basement in the late 1990s. I just wanted to build some bikes, impress my friends, challenge myself, and maybe make a few bucks. But within just a few years, Orange County Choppers had revolutionized the custom-bike business. When I started building bikes in my basement, Pro Street bikes were all the rage. Orange County Choppers, which had a more old-school look, changed all that. We not only turned heads, but we created a whole new market. And it all happened because I followed my passion and was true to myself and my principles. It can happen for you if you do the same thing: discover your passion, find a way to express it, and never give up.

As of early 2008, we started to build the first four bikes in the production line. We developed a marketing plan and set up a dealer network. Where it goes from there is anyone's guess. Where your business goes from here is totally up to you, as well. No one knows your business better than you. But once you figure out where it is, what you want it to be, and how you're going to get there, I think you'll be a success if you work hard, stay focused, and apply the principles and ideas that I've laid out in this book.

An Amazing Journey

My life and career has been a pretty amazing journey when you think about it. A kid from what was basically a broken home in New York: no role models, no teachers who believed in me. I overcame all of that—plus a wicked addiction to drugs and alcohol—because I figured out what my passion was, had a dream, and never let go of it. No matter what.

I very much believe that you're a product of your environment. Whatever your environment is, you become that. That's pretty much what you know. So I think that only having that to work with, I did pretty well. I took where I came from and turned it around to do the best that I could with what I had to work with. More importantly, I didn't want my children to have my childhood. I always tried to be a good provider and to overcome my perfections, as well as my imperfections.

And while my early life was defined by my addictions, my struggles didn't end simply because I got sober. It's like a person who's in prison. When they get out, they have to adapt to a different way of life. It's like a dog that's been kicked around most of its life, and then it has to adjust to a new home and an unfamiliar environment. It takes time to adjust to that new, unfamiliar way of life. Hopefully, you learn from your mistakes and become a better person.

The Legacy of OCC

My publisher asked me to talk about my legacy. This is always tough stuff for me. That's because I'm the guy who gets up every day, goes to work, tries to do his best, treats people the way he wants to be treated, and goes home at night and thinks about how he can do it better the next day. That's me. I'll never retire. My work is my life, because it's my passion.

But I think I know what my publisher wants, so here it goes. I hope I'll be remembered for the principles that I laid down in this book. Because they're not just words in a book; they're how I live my life—every minute of every day. I hope I'll be remembered for being honest, trustworthy, and dedicated. Someone who never sold out and always followed his passions and his dreams.

But most of all, I hope people will remember me as someone who did the best with what he had. Some people would look at my life and say that I've maximized my potential. I think I've done a lot more than that. Mainly because I came from nothing, I had no potential. Despite that, I always tried to make the most of myself and my life. And given where I started, I think I did pretty well. Personally, I hope people will remember me as someone who never forgot who he was or where he came from. With me, for better or worse, it was always, what you see is what you get.

I hope I'll also be remembered as a motorcycle guy, because that's who I am. I've always been a motorcycle man, and I will be a motorcycle man until the day I die. I was in the 1970s, and I still am today. I'm still nuts about bikes. I've never lost my passion for them. More importantly, I followed that passion and was lucky enough to make a pretty good living out of it.

As a father, I hope my kids will remember that, early in my life, I was a victim of circumstances. I didn't come from the greatest upbringing, and I did the best I could with what I had. I know in their eyes, I came up short sometimes. I accept that. Part of being an honest man is learning to accept responsibility for your mistakes. As a dad, I know I left a lot to be desired. But as with everything in my life, I was always trying to do my best.

Sticking to Your Principles

One of the principles when I first started Orange County Choppers was to never have my bikes or image used in connection with alcohol, tobacco, or naked women. I just felt that associating with those things would cheapen us and our brand. I wasn't going to do it. When we first went to Sturgis, the big bike rally held in South Dakota every summer, we were approached by one of the top motorcycle magazines in the country. They wanted to shoot a layout of our bikes. Unfortunately, I also knew that this particular mag was known for draping half-naked women across the bikes. We were at a crossroads. The shoot would've meant great exposure for us. It would also have meant going against one of our defining core principles.

After reading 200 pages of this book, I don't think I have to tell you what we did. And given the success of Orange County Choppers, I don't have to tell you how it all turned out. This wasn't the first time I'd been tempted to cut corners or temporarily look the other way when it came to my core principles. Over the years, there were lots of times when I could have made a quick buck. I never did it, and I'm glad I never did.

As for surviving this tough economy that we face in 2009, I'll tell you what I've been telling you throughout this book: Stick to your principles. They'll work for you in bad times as well as good. So in tough times, stay focused on your businesses. They don't run themselves. Be on top of your business, and know what's going on. And while you want to do the best by your employees, you also have to do the best by yourself and your business. This may require you to get rid of some people—valuable people you rely on and trust. But that's why they call them tough times. They don't make for some tough quarters in terms of sales and revenues, they sometimes require you to make some tough decisions. Use your brain, stick to your guns, and you'll do the right thing.

Find Your Dream

Now it's up to you. I've given you the blueprint. The roadmap, if you will. But figuring out what your dream is and what you want it to be is up to you. I can't do that for you. Once you figure out what your dream is, that's the easy part. The tough part will be making your dream a reality. You'll run into your own speed bumps, detours, and brick walls along the way. No doubt about it. And, like me, you'll have to figure out for yourself how to get around them or—if necessary—smash through them.

But if you hang in there, never lose sight of your dreams, surround yourself with good people, never stop growing, and stick to your word and your ideals, then your dreams can become reality, too. And, like me, you'll have *The Ride of a Lifetime.*